MONASTICISM:

Its Ideals and History

and

The Confessions of St. Augustine

Two Lectures

BY

ADOLF HARNACK

RECTOR OF, AND PROFESSOR OF CHURCH HISTORY IN, THE UNIVERSITY, AND
MEMBER OF THE ROYAL PRUSSIAN ACADEMY, BERLIN

Translated into English

BY

E. E. KELLETT, M.A., AND
F. H. MARSEILLE, Ph.D., M.A.

Wipf & Stock
PUBLISHERS
Eugene, Oregon

Wipf and Stock Publishers
199 West 8th Avenue, Suite 3
Eugene, Oregon 97401

Monasticism
Its Ideals and History and the Confessions of St. Augustine
By Harnack, Adolf
ISBN: 1-59244-592-6
Publication date 3/17/2004
Previously published by Williams and Norgate, 1911

TRANSLATORS' PREFACE.

THE larger works of Professor Harnack have long been known in England, and have established his fame as one of the foremost leaders of contemporary religious thought. His minor works display on a smaller scale the same historic sense, the same wide and profound learning, and the same sympathy with varying points of view, which characterise his more ambitious productions; and at the same time are perhaps capable of appealing to a wider circle of readers. Two of the most popular and interesting of these, *Das Mönchthum* and *Augustin's Confessionen*, are here offered to the English public. The version of the former is made from the fifth German edition.

The translators desire to express their best thanks to the Rev. Dr Taylor, Rector of Winchcombe, for several valuable suggestions.

CONTENTS.

.

Monasticism

THE Christian creeds, different as they may
be from one another, unite in demanding
that faith must exhibit itself in a Christ-like
life : that, in fact, Christianity only comes by
its own where it issues in a characteristic life.
A genuinely Christian life is the common
ideal of Christendom. But what is the
nature of that life to be? Here the ways
part. The diversity of creeds among us is,
in the last analysis, as much due to the
difference of beliefs as to that of the ideals
of life engendered by the belief. All other
distinctions, in a religious sense, are unessen-
tial, or derive from hence their importance
and their meaning. It is not only theolo-

gical wrangling, nor priestly lust of power, nor national diversities, to which schism in the Church is due—they have had their share, it is true, in originating it, and still help to maintain it; but what has really divided the Church, and given permanence to that division, is the variety of answers to the question,—What is the ideal of life? It is with the relations of groups not otherwise than with those of individuals. Not theoretic opinions, but feelings and aims, sunder and unite.

If we ask either the Roman or the Greek Church wherein the most perfect Christian life consists, both alike reply : in the service of God, to the abnegation of all the good things of this life — property, marriage, personal will, and honour ; in a word, in the religious renunciation of the world, that is, in Monasticism. The true monk is the true and most perfect Christian. Monasticism, then, is not in the Catholic Churches a more or less accidental phenomenon alongside of others ;

but, as the Churches are to-day, and as they have for centuries understood the Gospel, it is an institution based on their essential nature; it is *the* Christian life. We may therefore be allowed to expect that in the ideals of monasticism the ideals of the Church will be expressed, and in the history of monasticism the history of the Church.

But is it possible for monasticism to have varying ideals? Is a history of monasticism possible? Is it not condemned to pass through history in the everlasting repetition of a grand monotony? Of what variety are the ideals of poverty, chastity, and resolute flight from the world capable? What sort of development can *they* experience or introduce who have turned their back not on the world only, but on its changing forms—that is, on its history? Is not the renunciation of the world essentially the abnegation of all development and of all history? Or, if it has not been so in fact, is not a *history* of monkish ideals from the very first a protest against the very conception of monasticism ? It appears so—and it perhaps not merely appears so. But the history of the West shows even the most careless observer that monasticism has had its history, not only external but internal, full of the mightiest changes and the mightiest results. What a chasm divides the silent anchorite of the desert, who for a lifetime has looked no man in the face, from the monk who imposed his commands upon a world! And between these extremes are the hundreds of figures, peculiar and distinct, and yet monks, all inspired and dominated by the idea of a renunciation! And yet more, all stirrings of the heart, the most passionate and the most delicate, meet us in that world of renunciation. Art, poetry, science, have found in it a fostermother ; nay, the beginnings of our civilisation are a chapter from the history of monasticism. Was all this only possible to a monasticism that abandoned its ideals, or do its most special ideals admit of such effects ? Does renunciation constitute a second world and a second history, like the usual world and the usual history, but purer and greater, or must it transform the world into a wilderness? Is the true monasticism that which sees in the world the temple of God, and which perceives with rapture in silent nature the breath of the divine spirit; or is that the true monasticism which maintains that the world with its nature and its history is the devil's? Both these watchwords resound to us from the kingdom of renunciation: which of them is authentic, having the sanction of historical truth? In monasticism the individual has been released from the bonds of society and custom, and raised to a noble self-reliance and humanity; in monasticism, again, it has been enslaved to narrowness, empty barrenness, and servile dependence. Is the original ideal to be blamed for the one or praised for the other?

Such questions, and others like them, arise here. The evangelical Christian has in their

correct answer no merely historical interest.
Even if he be convinced that Christian
perfection is not to be sought in the forms of
monasticism, he has yet to test that system
and establish its true character. Only then
is it in truth overcome when a better can
be set above the best it has to offer. But
he who disparagingly casts it aside understands it not. He who understands it will
recognise how much there is to learn from it.
Nay, he will be able to learn from it not as
from an opponent but as from a friend ; not
only not to the injury of his evangelical
standpoint, but rather to its advantage. Let
us then seek to gain a true appreciation of
monasticism by means of an historical survey.

I.

Monasticism is not as old as the Church.
It is true that the Church of the fourth
century, in which it took shape, thought it

found even in the apostolic age essentially
similar institutions ; but the models which
some persons have invoked, and still invoke,
as precedents belong chiefly to legend. Yet
the ancient Church was not wholly in error
in its view. The idea of detachment, of
forming close associations within the congregation, and of practising a special
renunciation, could obviously not occur to
individuals in the earliest decades of the
Church's existence. But those who felt
themselves driven by the Spirit of God to
dedicate their whole life to the spread of the
Gospel, as a rule gave up all their possessions,
and wandered in voluntary poverty from one
city to another as Apostles or Evangelists of
Christ. Others, renouncing property and
marriage, devoted themselves wholly to the
service of the poor and needy of the congregation. These apostolic men were doubtless,
when monasticism sought for its origins in
the apostolic age, again remembered. And
further, all Christians, so far as they were

serious, were equally dominated by the belief
that the world and its history had but
a short span allowed before the end. Where
this expectation is a living force, life, as
usually lived, can no longer maintain an
independent value, however conscientiously
a man may recognise the calls of duty. The
Apostle Paul, under special circumstances,
repeatedly and expressly drove these home
to the hearts of his congregations. For
this reason he has been claimed on the
Evangelical side as an opponent of monkery
and all ascetic forms of Christianity; for
he was the champion of Christian freedom.
But we must not forget that even he has
laid it down, in reference to worldly goods,
that it is more advantageous to the Christian
to renounce them, and that such is also
the teaching of the Gospels. Yet by this
that which has developed itself as monasticism
is neither recommended nor commanded.
Christ laid on us no heavy burdens as a new
and painful law; and still less did He see

salvation in asceticism as such. He Himself did not live as an ascetic; but He set before us a perfect simplicity and purity of thought, and a detachment of heart which, in abnegation and tribulation, in the possession and use of earthly goods, should remain unalterably the same. The simplest and hardest command in the Law—the love of God and of our neighbour—He set at the head of all, and opposed to all ceremonial sanctity and to all over-refined morality. He bade us take up each his own cross, that is, the sufferings which God appoints, and follow Him. The following of Jesus, in which is realised the search for the Kingdom of God and His righteousness, includes in itself the renunciation of all that clogs or hinders. But monasticism in later times tried so to adapt itself to the decisive Evangelical command 'Deny thyself,' that it fixed the bounds of denial without regard to individual disposition or calling.

When, in the first century and in the beginning of the second, Christianity took up its mission in the Græco-Roman world, it was welcomed by those susceptible to its influence as the message of renunciation and of resurrection. The latter offered the delivering hope, and the former demanded the severance from the world of sin and sensuality. The first Christians saw in heathendom, in its idolatry, in its public life, even in its political constitution, the Kingdom of Satan actually realised; and they demanded therefore renunciation of that world. But to them it was no irreconcilable contradiction that the earth is the Lord's, guided and ruled by Him, and that it yet lies at the same time under the devastating rule of Satan. Again, they knew themselves as citizens of a world to come, upon which they were soon to enter. One who thus believes may easily make light of all that is around him, without falling into the attitude which is called pessimism, and which at best is the mental habit of the disappointed and wearied hero. He will keep the joy of 'life';

for he wishes for nothing more earnestly than to live, and he will gladly surrender himself to the death which leads to life. There is no room for the abnegation of joy where there is a living belief that God made and rules the world, or where it is clearly realised that not a sparrow falls without our Father. True it is that the imagination was then most actively stirred by the conception that the present course of the world stands forfeit to judgment, inasmuch as the trail of the serpent is over the whole creation which thus deserves destruction; but this world was nevertheless recognised as the sphere of God's kingdom, and thus worthy of a transforming renewal. Christianity had to take up the struggle alike with the gross and with the refined sensuality of heathenism; and Christianity, as has been well said, exhausted all her energies in proclaiming the great message: "Ye are not animals, but immortal souls; not the slaves of the flesh and of matter, but the lords of your flesh, and

servants of the living God only." All ideals
of culture must fall into the background
till this message is believed. Better that
man should regard marriage, eating and
drinking, nay, his human side in itself as
impure, than that he should *make* these
things impure by sensual degeneracy. No
new principle can assert itself in this world
of sluggishness and custom unless it applies
the keenest criticism to the condition of the
present time and makes the most exacting
demands upon us. Such demands the oldest
Christianity did make ; but soon arose the
question what their theoretic foundations were
to be, and to what extent they were to be
binding.

II.

So early as the beginning of the second
century, a motley crowd of enquirers and believers began to knock at the doors of the

Christian churches. Among them were men —usually called Gnostics—who were nourished and bewildered by the old and newest wisdom of the mysteries, but who were at the same time captivated by the evangelical message, and by the purity of the Christian life. They sought to define wherein consisted the essence of the Christian religion as a cognition of God and of the world; and they imagined they had established the true meaning of the Gospel—a meaning unknown to the common herd—God as the Lord and Creator of spirits, but over against Him from all eternity the realm of matter, of the finite and sensuous, which as such is evil : the human spirit a spark of the divine, but fatally enveloped by its enemy, the material world ; the redemption by Christ a release of the spirit from the body, and the restoration of pure spirituality. Hence the moral task—perfect asceticism, flight from daemonic nature, union with the original source of spirit by gnosis and knowledge. In the strife with this doctrine,

which was Greek, but endeavoured to natural-
ise itself as Christian, and in the strife with
Marcionism, which in its practical teachings
was closely allied with Gnosticism, the Church
passed through the first great crisis in her
history. She was victorious. This appar-
ently attractive attempt to find a philoso-
phic basis for her own criticism of the
present world she rejected as false and foreign
to herself. She recognised in these doctrines
the recurrence of daemonic, that is, of heathen
conceptions; and condemned as secular
Gnostic Christianity, with its asceticism and
its lofty proclamations of the nobility and
value of the Spirit. Nor only this, but she
refused to know anything of a pretended
higher esoteric Christianity for the ' spiritual ' :
as against the Gnostic distinction of two
Christian ideals, she took her stand, though
with some hesitation, on the demand of a single
and universally attainable Christian order of
life. From the end of the second century it
was for ever established in the Church that

the belief in an essential dualism of God and the World, Spirit and Nature, was irreconcilable with Christianity, and that therefore all asceticism which rests on that dualism was equally irreconcilable therewith. The doctrine, indeed, continued to be taught that the present course of the world and the future time stand in opposition, that the earth has fallen under the dominion of demons. But it was God himself that made the surrender, and yielded the world to the devil. Yet He will show His omnipotence at the Last Judgment: nay, He shows it already in the victory of the faithful over the demons. The earth is the Lord's, but it is temporarily governed by the wicked angels ; the world is good, but the life of the world is bad. It was thus that the theory of dualism was overthrown; by decrying it in ' theology,' and by seeking the explanation of evil in the freedom of the creature, which was a necessity in God's plan. Nevertheless the enemy that lurks here may indeed be defeated, but he cannot be annihilated.

He found secret allies even in many theologians
of authority, who knew how in subtle fashion
to combine dualism with a belief in God the
Almighty Creator.   Under the most various
disguises he again and again appears in the
history of Christianity; but he has been
obliged to mask his features.   As an open
enemy he is seen no more.

Before this first crisis was at an end, a
second arose to confront the Church.   From
the middle of the second century the conditions of the external position of Christendom began to alter more and more.   Hitherto
it had been scattered over the Roman Empire
in a few small communities.   These had been
provided only with the most necessary
forms of political organisation, as few and
loose as were required by a religious union
based on superhuman hopes, strict discipline,
and brotherly affection.   But a change was at
hand.   The Church received large multitudes
which stood in need as much of a belated
discipline—education and forbearance—as of

a political guidance. The prospect of an approaching end of the world no longer, as of old, dominated all hearts. In place of the original enthusiasm there arose more and more a sober conviction or, perhaps, even a mere theoretical belief and a submissive acceptance. There were many who did not *become* Christians, but, finding themselves Christians, remained so. They were too strongly impressed by Christianity to leave it, and too little impressed to be Christian indeed. Pure religious enthusiasm began to wane, old ideals received a new form, and the self-reliance and responsibility of individuals grew weaker. The 'priests and kings of God' began to clamour for priests, and to come to terms with the kings of the earth. Those who once had prided themselves on being filled with the Spirit, no longer traced that Spirit so actively in themselves, and sought to recognise it in symbols of faith, in holy books, in mysteries, and in forms of Church order. The differences, again, in the social status of the 'brethren' began to assert themselves. Christians were already to be found in all callings—in the Emperor's palace, among the officials, in the workshops of the handicraftsmen, and in the studies of the learned, among the free, and among the enslaved. Were all these to continue in their occupations? Should the Church make the decisive stride into the world, enter into its relations, comply with its forms, recognise, as far as anyhow possible, its ordinances, meet its requirements; or should she remain, as she had been at first, a congregation of religious enthusiasts, separate and distinct from the world, and influencing the world only by a direct missionary propaganda? From the latter half of the second century the Church found herself confronted with the dilemma, either to begin a world-mission on a grand scale by effectively entering the Roman social system—of course, to the rejection of her original equipment and force —or to retain these, to keep the original forms of life, but remain a small and insignificant sect, scarcely intelligible to one in a thousand, incapable of saving and educating whole nations. This was the question—thus much we can assert to-day, obscurely as it could then be perceived. It was a great crisis, and—it was not the worst Christians who cried a halt. Now for the first time were voices heard in the Church, warning bishops and congregations against the advancing secularisation, holding up to the secular Christian those well-known sentences about the imitation of Christ in their literal sternness, and demanding a return to pristine simplicity and purity. Then once again arose, loud and penetrating, the cry to establish life on the ground of the expectation of the Lord's speedy return. There were congregations which, led by their bishops, withdrew to the desert; there were congregations which sold all their possessions in order to be able to meet the coming Christ, having laid aside every weight; there

were voices that cried that Christians should
forsake the broad way and seek the narrow
way and the strait gate. The Church herself, impelled rather by circumstances than
by a free movement, decided otherwise. She
entered the world-state by the open door in
order to establish herself permanently in it,
to preach Christianity in its streets, to bring
it the word of the Gospel, but—to leave it in
possession of all except its gods. And she
equipped herself with all the good things she
could get from it, without marring the
elasticity of the structure within which she
was now establishing herself. With the aid of
its philosophy she created her new Christian
theology; its constitution she exploited in
order to give herself a firm organisation; its
jurisprudence, trade, intercourse, art, handi-
craft she pressed into her service; even from
its ritual she learned to profit. Thus it is
that at the middle of the third century we
find the Church furnished with all the forces
that a State and its culture could offer her,

entering on all the relations of life, and ready
for any concession which did not concern her
creed. With this equipment she undertook
and carried through a world-mission on a large
scale. And those old-fashioned, those more
serious believers, who protested against this
secularised Church in the name of the Gospel,
who aimed at gathering for their God a holy
congregation, regardless of numbers and of
circumstances ? These could no longer remain
in the great Church ; and the majority of
them, to provide a foundation for their stricter
demands, claimed to have received a new
and final revelation of God in Phrygia, and
thus hastened the breach. They severed
themselves, or were severed, from the Church.
But, as usually happens, they had in the very
struggle grown narrower and more one-sided.
If, in the earlier times, a lofty enthusiasm had
called forth as of itself stern forms of life, these
now, minutely regulated, were to conserve and
beget that original life. They became forma-
lists in the direction of their lives, which after

all were but little stricter than those of their
adversaries, and they became haughty in their
assertion of a 'pure' Christianity. Secular
Christianity they despised as a mongrel, mechanical, unspiritual Christianity. In this 'sect'
of the Montanists of the Empire, and in the
related but older and yet more uncompromising
Encratites, with their shrinking from the world,
their more strictly ordered fasts and prayers,
their distrust of the priestly office, of Church
polity, of all property, and even of marriage,
some have seen the forerunners of later
monasticism. Nor is this view incorrect, if
we look merely at the motives of the two
movements; but in other respects there
remains a great difference. Monasticism pre-
supposes the comparative legitimacy of the
secular Church ; these Montanists denied it
altogether. The device of a double morality
in the Church may have existed in embryo ;
but it did not, at the beginning of the third
century, dominate the entire conception of
the Christian life, as is shown by the very

fact that Montanism severed itself from the Church. True, the Church set a value on its ' confessors,' its ' virgins,' its celibates, its God-serving widows—provided they remained true to her communion—and that value became higher the oftener she discovered by experience that they tended to grow distrustful of the ' great society.' But these spiritual aristocrats were as yet no more monks than were the Montanists. Again, monasticism raised a way of life into a principle, which in the first instance was based, not on the prospect of the impending revelation of the kingdom of Christ, but on the idea of a perfect enjoyment of God here and of immortality yonder. Monasticism had necessarily to make an effort to fly from the world ; Montanism did not expressly require a flight from that which its enthusiastic hope regarded as a thing already overcome.

III.

Bᴜᴛ let us return to the Church of the third century. These zealots had indeed a right to criticise her; for the great dangers which they foresaw if the Church should enter into relations with the world-state did indeed appear. The saying of the apostle, 'To the Jews a Jew, to the Greeks a Greek,' noble as it was, was yet a dangerous maxim. The tradition of centuries has accustomed us to date the first secularisation of the Church from the time when, under Constantine, she began to be a State-Church. This tradition is false; the Church was already—in the middle of the third century—to a high degree secularised. Not that she had denied her traditional dogmas, or renounced her characteristic nature; but she had dangerously lowered her standard of life; and the apparatus of external culture with which she had enriched herself had turned to her spiritual harm. True, she was externally more firmly and solidly compacted

than ever—she had become a state within a
state—but the strong band that held her
together was no longer religious hopes or
brotherly love, but a hierarchic system which
threatened to stifle not only Christian freedom
and independence, but also the very sense of
brotherhood. Her doctrine already rivalled
the admired systems of the philosophers ; but
she had herself become too deeply imbued with
their philosophy ; her aims were deranged, her
methods disturbed. Especially had she been
influenced by the latest, posthumous system of
Greek thought, Neoplatonism. By that which
Neoplatonism lent her, she sought to hide the
gaps caused long since by the loss or the change
of her purely religious ideals. But the supramundane God of Neoplatonism was not the
God of the Gospel, and the Neoplatonic
promise of release from the world of sense was
far different from the original Christian hope of
salvation. Yet the theologians who studied
or opposed it were subdued to its influence,
and their own conceptions became imper-

c

ceptibly affected thereby.   Yet further, the
tendency to conform to the State grew ever
more manifest.   It is true that Christianity
sought to support the State ; but she demanded
its support in return, and did more to gain
it over than she ought to have done.   Lastly,
the Church at length proved unable to maintain
even her abated claims on the moral life of individuals ; she was often constrained to content
herself with a minimum, a mere external obedience to her institutions and forms of worship.
On the other hand, she had attained this one
point, that no Christian should wantonly assail
her claim to be *the* Christian society ; she had
established the dogma that her organised
community, with its bishops, its divine
gifts, its sacred books, its worship, was the
authentic and genuine foundation of Christ
and His apostles, outside of which there was
no salvation.   Such was the Christian Church
at the end of the third century and the
beginning of the fourth.   To this she had
come, not without her own fault.   Yet we

ought to say, that while it is easy to measure
this Church by the standard of apostolic times
or by an imagined prototype, and to censure
her gross secularisation, it is yet unjust to
leave out of sight the historic conditions which
influenced her. What she kept was, after all,
not merely a remnant that she could not lose,
nor a ruin that was not worth the preserving,
but the old Gospel—though a Gospel dressed
in the hulls and trappings of the time, and
bereft of the vigorous claim to regulate the
whole of life from within.

But this Church was no longer in a position
to give peace to all that came to her, and
to shelter them from the world. She could
promise a peace beyond the grave, but peace
in the storms of this life she could not secure.
Then began the great upheaval. Ascetics, even
anchorites, there had already been in the great
Church, no less than evangelists without
property and travelling from place to place.
In the course of the third century, there may
already have been a few instances of indi-

viduals, tired of the world, fleeing into the
desert; nay, they may here and there have
actually joined together for common life. At
the opening of the new century their number
increased. They fled not the world only, but
worldliness in the Church; yet they did not
therefore flee *from* the Church. Honours and
riches, wife and children, they renounced in
order to shun pleasure and sin, to give
themselves up to the enjoyment of the contemplation of God, and to consecrate life by
the preparation for death. And rightly, in so
far as the dominant theology also taught that
the ideal of the Christian life consisted
precisely in this practising for death, and
again in that absorption in God in which man
forgets his existence, and mortifies his body
all but to death, in order to absorb himself in
the very vision of the heavenly and eternal.
This was the universal view of the wise,
and they were in earnest. Yet further,
no age, perhaps, was ever more deeply penetrated with the idea that the fashion of this

world passeth away, that life is not worth
living. In actual fact, a great epoch in
human history was passing away. The Roman
Empire, the old world, hastened to die, and
fearful were its death-bed agonies. Sedition,
bloodshed, poverty, pestilence within; without,
the barbarous hordes on all sides. What was
to be set against all this? No longer the
power of a self-sufficient State, or the force of
a uniform and tried ideal of civilisation, but
an Empire falling asunder, hardly held together by a decaying and disintegrated
culture; and that culture itself hollow and
untrue, in which scarcely a single man could
keep a good conscience, or a free natural mind,
or a clean hand. But nowhere was the inner
unreality of all relations more necessarily felt
than at the centres of culture, and especially
at Alexandria. Is it then wonderful that
precisely there, in Lower Egypt, hermit life
took its rise? The Egyptian people had the
longest and richest history of all known
nations; and even under the dominion of

foreigners, under the sword of the Roman conqueror, Egypt was the land of toil, and its capital had remained the school of culture. But now the hour of the nation had come. It was then that monasticism, as a mighty movement, there took its origin ; not much later we meet it on the east coast of the Mediterranean, and on the banks of the Euphrates. Attempts have in recent times been made to explain its rise from specifically heathen influences on Christianity in Egypt ; but the question has not been sufficiently carefully examined, though we ought to be thankful for the proof that older analogous phenomena existed in the domain of the Egyptian religion. External influence was here not stronger, but probably even weaker than in any other province of Christian life and thought. It is true that, after the general fashion of mankind, Christianity at every stage of its development elaborated and proclaimed as the highest that ideal of life which necessity imposed. But here social,

political, and religious pressure combined with
a long existent Christian ideal which soon
passed for that of the Apostles.

There were, however, diverse conditions,
and correspondingly different stages which
preceded the growth of monasticism. Though
the main agent was an ascetic instinct, born
in the Church from heathen origins, the
instinct to free the spirit from its many
tyrants, to overcome both gross and refined
egoism, to lead the soul to God—yet there
was combined with it an ascetic ideal which
was less related than opposed to that impulse.
In the Alexandrian catechumen school, which
in the third century was the chief fountain
of ecclesiastical theology, the fundamental
ideas of the idealist Greek moralists since
Socrates were all taken up and closely studied.
But these moralists had long since turned
the Socratic rule 'Know thyself' into
various directions for a right guidance of life.
Most of these directions endeavoured to
divert the true 'Wise Man' from absorption

in the service of daily life and from " taking
up the burden of public duty." They
asserted that " there could be nothing more
fitting or appropriate for the spirit than
a care for itself, which, not looking without,
nor busying itself with external things, but
turning inwardly on itself, devotes its essence
to itself, and thus practises righteousness."
Here was taught the doctrine that the Wise
Man, standing no longer in need of anything, is nearest to the Godhead, because, in
full command of his richly endowed Ego, and
in peaceful contemplation of the world, he has
his share in the highest good. There it was
proclaimed that the spirit, freed from the
dominion of sense and living in constant
meditation on eternal ideas, becomes at length
worthy to behold the invisible and is itself
made divine. It was this flight from the
world which the ecclesiastical philosophers of
Alexandria, and above all, Origen, taught their
pupils. We have but to read the panegyric of
Gregory Thaumaturgus on his great master,

to see where are to be found the prototypes
of this doctrine of the flight from the
world, so belauded in the theologians. No
one can deny that this form of renunciation
involves a specific secularisation of Christianity,
or that the self-sufficient Wise Man is almost
diametrically opposed to the humble soul.
But neither can anyone fail to recognise
that both admitted of material realisation
in endless diversities of form ; and by this
very diversity were liable to pass over into
one another. And in this sense specially
is Origen himself to be counted among
the real founders of monasticism. True,
what even he in his ethics brought to full
expression was not merely the Stoic or
Neoplatonic ideal, nor did he realise it in
his life. Rather, all the ethical tendencies
of the past, the Christian included, meet
in him. For the position of the Egyptian
theologians in the history of the world is
this—and they all were forerunners or else
pupils of Origen—that, alike in the domain

of dogma and in that of the discipline of
the Christian life, they unified the manifold
gains of the existing forms of knowledge and
practical rules, and threw over them the
ægis of Revelation. It is thus that they
became the fathers of all those parties in the
Greek Church, that afterwards arose and
contended with each other. As Origen could
with equal right be claimed both by Arianism
and by Orthodoxy, so he can be made answerable with equal justice for the peculiar
secularisation of the theology of the Church
and for the monastic inclinations first of the
theologians and then of the laity. The same
man who maintained the desirability of a
lasting peace between Christianity and the
State on earth, and predicted its realisation,
simultaneously wished to see established, in
the shadow of a universal peace, the cell of
the learned monk, pious and self-absorbed.
But the man that was not pious *and learned*,
had yet in his faith an inexhaustible object
of contemplation. Thus the demand, in

truth, is made upon all Christians; yet, in a Christianity that was ever growing more indifferent, almost two generations went by before these ideas asserted their force, and they never became the most decisive ideas to the masses. Rare, indeed, were unions of monks, such as those which were modelled by Hieracas, the pupil of Origen, on the plan supplied by Origen himself. Distress and disgust with the everyday life started the movements as if with an irresistible natural force; and the Church of Constantine drove into solitude and the desert those who wished to devote themselves to religion.

About 340 A.D. the movement had already become powerful. There must by that time have been thousands of hermits. The beginnings of monasticism proper, as of every great historical phenomenon, are shrouded in legend; and it is to legend, not to history, that we owe the memory of pretended founders. It is no longer possible to discriminate between fact and fancy. But we

are certain on two points; and these are
sufficient to enable us to discern and rightly
judge the movement in its general outlines.
We know the original ideal, and we can
measure the extent of the renunciation. The
ideal was an undisturbed contemplation of
God; the means, absolute denial of the good
things of life—and among them of Church
communion. Not only was the world, in
every sense of the word, to be avoided, but
the secularised Church as well. Not that her
teachings were held insufficient, her ordinances
inappropriate, her divine gift indifferent; but
her foundation was regarded as insecure,
and men doubted not to make up for the loss
of her sacramental advantages by asceticism
and unceasing contemplation of what is holy.

And what was the attitude of the secular
Church herself to the movement? Could she
bear to see her members venturing to release
themselves from her direct guidance, and
striking out a path of salvation outside her
own control? Could she permit her sons,

even if they did not directly attack her
ordinances, to cast on them the shadow of
a suspicion? She did not, and she could
not, hesitate for a moment. She did the one
thing left to secure her safety, in expressly
approving the movement, nay, in bearing
testimony that it realised the original ideal of
the Christian life. The dread of inevitably
losing themselves in the whirl of life, the
disgust with that life, so empty and common,
the prospect of a lofty good, had driven these
men out of the world, and the Church made a
virtue of necessity. Nor could she help doing
so; for the more deeply she became involved
in the world, in politics, and in culture, the
more loudly and impressively had she preached
what monasticism now practised.

It is one of the most striking historical
facts that the Church, precisely at the time
when she was becoming more and more a
legal and sacramental institution, threw out
an ideal of life which could be realised, not in
herself, but only alongside of herself. The

more deeply she became compromised with the world, the higher, the more superhuman became her ideal. She herself taught that the loftiest aim of the Gospel was the contemplation of God; and she herself knew no surer way to this contemplation than flight from the world. Yet this line of thought appears in her only as the incongruous complement of the shallow morality to which she had reduced Christianity. Though her aims were actually directed to subjecting every thing to her poor moral rules and her ordinances of worship, yet her own theology tended in the opposite direction. Monasticism, unable to find satisfaction in 'theology,' seriously accepted the view that Christianity is a *religion*, and demands from the individual a surrender of his life. But it is an evidence of the extraordinary force with which the Church had established herself in the minds of men, that monasticism, on its first appearance, did not venture, like the Montanists, to criticise the Church, or to brand her path as a departure from the truth. If we consider what an enthusiasm, nay, what a fanaticism, speedily developed itself in the monastic communities, we shall be astonished to observe how few and ineffective were the attacks on the Church—even though they were not altogether absent. Hardly a single man demanded a reform of Christianity generally. The movement might well have proved a revolution for the secular Church, yet in truth it did not turn her paths aside. It is true that men conceived a strong distrust of the priestly office ; how many fled when an attempt was made to impose that office on them ! But reverence for it did not die out : it was only its dangers that men feared. Here and there a strain may have been visible between priests and monks, but in those cases it was the *person*, not the office, that was contemned.

———

IV.

BUT let us not anticipate. Thousands had
gone out, and the reputation of sanctity, dissatisfaction with the world, or dislike of work,
enticed thousands after them. Of inducements
to a monastic life there were many, especially
since the establishment of a State Church,
when a real or affected enthusiasm no longer
led to martyrdom. Even about the middle of
the fourth century there was a motley crew of
anchorites in the desert. Some had gone out
in order really to make atonement and to
become saints; others to pose as such. Some
fled society and its vices; others their calling
and its toils. Some were simple-hearted and
of indomitable will; others were sick of the
whirl of life. In the one case the hermit
desired to be rich in knowledge and true joy,
and to devote his life to 'philosophy' in
peaceful mental enjoyment; in the other he
desired to become poor both in mind and in
body, despising reason and learning. We

have touching confessions of both kinds; but the complaints of the temptations of the world and of the inroads of sense resound louder than those of the selfishness of the heart. And alongside of the silent penitent we soon find the lawless enthusiast. The latter required a fetter; the other two required an organisation. And organisation was soon to appear; a life in common emerges into our view. We find it in two forms: colonies of cremites on the one hand and actual monasteries on the other. Rules were laid down, often very severe. They exhibit not only the sternness of asceticism, but also, even thus early, gross excesses which were to be punished, and simultaneously, here and there in the monastic colonies, an awakening fanaticism which passed all bounds. Thus early do we come across men who remind us of the Mad Dervishes of whom Oriental travellers still tell us. But even among genuine monks we observe, even in the fourth century, the most important differences. True, the fundamental rules of exclusive life with

D

God, of poverty and chastity, and, in the
monasteries, of obedience, are in all cases the
same. But how differently did they work out
in practice! To name only one point : some,
full of thankfulness to have escaped from a
false and artificial culture, discover in solitude
what they had never seen—Nature. Into her
they gradually grow ; her beauty they search
out and extol. From hermits of the fourth
century we have pictures of nature such as antiquity seldom produced. Like happy children
they tried to live to their God in His garden.
In that garden they see the tree of knowledge
—no longer forbidden—and thus solitude
becomes to them a Paradise ; no curse lies
upon their toil, for to know is to be blessed.
But the others—they understood asceticism
otherwise. Not only culture, but nature, is
to be shunned ; not only social ordinances,
but humanity itself. Everything that can be
an occasion of sin—and what is there that
cannot ?—must be cast aside ; all joy, all
knowledge, all that is lofty in man. And

what was the result? One man starved
himself to death; a second ranged to and
fro like a beast of the desert; a third plunged
into the mud of the Nile and let himself be
tortured by insects; a fourth, half-naked, the
sport of wind and weather, spent years in
silence on a pillar. Thus was the flesh to be
subjected and crucified; thus was man to
gain peace of soul in the contemplation of
God: he was to be pure and to keep silence.
But these men themselves were fain to confess
that the sense of peace came upon them but
rarely and for a moment. In its place came
terrible phantasies, which took shape as con-
crete realities. And contemporaries eagerly
listened to accounts of such experiences. The
ageing world was enraptured with this refine-
ment of renunciation, and with the wild
dreams of monks dwelling miserably in the
desert. Men to whom courage and will to
perform were wanting, sought to enjoy these
emotions at least in fancy. Story-tellers in
monks' dress made novels and tales out of

the actual or visionary experiences of silent penitents. Now appeared a new species of literature of the strangest kind, that of monasticism, and in its pages whole centuries found edification. This is one of the ways in which the secular Church repaid the deeds of that stern heroism which her own neglect was constantly calling into exercise.

But of the two forms of monasticism here sketched in outline, which can claim a direct descent from Græco-Christian ancestry? Which ideal, considered under historical and religious relations, was the genuine one? That of the brethren who joyed in God and Nature, and devoted their lives in quiet seclusion to the knowledge of God and the world; or that of the heroic penitents? It is not merely to judge by results to say the latter alone. For, in considering the former, we must attend to the close relation in which it stands to the classical ideal of the philosopher; nor this alone. Let us for a moment put ourselves into the historic standpoint. The highest ideal—in the universal belief of the time—can only be realised outside of the world, outside of any calling; it lies hidden in asceticism. Asceticism is indeed a means to an end; but at the same time it is an end in itself: for it contains in itself the assurance that the penitent shall attain to the vision of God. If these pre-positions are correct, then all is mere com-promise that hinders the struggle *à outrance*; then not culture only, but nature, history, in a word, all purposed moral activity must be put aside as imperfect and harmful. *Then* it becomes essential to dare the glorious attempt, to free oneself from nature, from culture, nay, from the world of social morality, in order to be able in this way to form in oneself a pure type of the religious man. Here we reach the actual secret, but here also we touch the boundary of the old Greek view of Christianity. Even before the secular Church there floated as the highest ideal a vision of the religious life which raises man, even here on earth, beyond all the conditions of his existence—including the historical and social conditions. Not as if these were indifferent, or as if their opposite were equally right. But hitherto Christianity had been unable to realise any new moral life in a community, and the moral standards of the old life were outworn, useless, or no longer to be found. It was only a natural consequence that thus the more serious spirits—who yet were no reformers—should have felt the moral ordinances, in their degenerate state, as barriers essentially no better than the elementary conditions of human existence. Thus is a Christian ideal sketched out which is ostensibly purely religious—I should like to say supra-moral. It is not by way of historically founded social ordinances, or of activity with a moral end, that the Christian faith is to come by its own; but by way of the renunciation of everything human; that is, by the extremest asceticism. Thus shall we anticipate our coming share in the divine nature. This is, even to-day, the ideal aim of Greek Christendom, so far as it is not fossilised or diverted by Western influences : we cannot deny to it our sympathy if we think of the low level of so-called Christian morality above which, since it knows no better, it strives to rise. But it is a flight as barren as it is magnificent. For what do we now perceive ? On the one side, a secular Church, subjected to the State and so knitted with the national life as to be indistinguishable from it ; essentially a civilising agent, with but the smallest influence on the moral life of its members, and no longer pursuing definite aims of its own. On the other, a monasticism without historic aims, and therefore without historic development. To-day—a few modern and perhaps hopeful phenomena being disregarded—it remains essentially what it was in the days of the first Byzantine Emperors. Even external regulations have scarcely altered. True, the type of Simeon Stylites is extinct; such types cannot conquer in the struggle for existence; but the *cause* of Simeon has been victorious, and so far has Stylites prevailed that even to-day the extremest asceticism counts for the best, and above all in this point, that Greek monasticism has seldom succeeded in giving itself up to purposed toil in the service of the Church or of humanity. The Greek monks— of course with venerable exceptions—to-day as a thousand years ago, live "in silent contemplation and blissful ignorance." To work they give only just as much attention as is necessary for a livelihood; but even now the unlearned monk is to the learned necessarily a reproach, the avoider of nature a reproach to the nature worshipper; still must conscience smite the working hermit when he sees the brother who neither toils nor spins nor speaks, but waits in solitary contemplation and mortification for the holy light of God to shine at last on him. As in the fifth century, so now, the rift continues between the regulars and the seculars. It is true that the higher dignitaries of the Church are chosen from the regulars—monasticism has even given Emperor and court a temporary or lasting ugly varnish—but the mutual relations have remained the same. The monastery stands alongside the Church, not in it ; and it cannot be otherwise. What could it do for the Church which itself renounces every task of its own ? The one thing in which it takes a living interest is the worship of the Church : it paints pictures of saints ; occasionally it illuminates books. But even from worship it is allowed to emancipate itself. The hermit who for years shuns the communion of the Church is not merely tolerated by her; he is admired. Nay, she cannot help admiring him ; for he realises the ideal to which she herself cannot attain—her *higher* ideal, I mean ; for she now has two—that of asceticism and that of worship. He to whom the gift or the power is not given of attaining God by asceticism, may yet reach Him by becoming imbued with the holy mysteries of divine service. Salvation may be obtained by the worship of the Church if we join in it with piety, and if Church duties are duly performed. Monasticism has never attacked this theory, but rather supported it ; and rightly, for indirectly she was benefited by it.

For short periods the monastery approached the secular Church ; and the latter, again, sought to take it into her service. For short periods, also, the attempt succeeded. The great Synods of the fifth to the seventh centuries provide examples. The dogmas which these Synods established arose in part from monkish fancy, and were defended by monkish arguments and monkish blows. But as the Bishops grew more cautious they shrank from calling the fanaticism of the monks to their aid ; for whenever the latter took part in the strife there arose in due consequence revolution, war, and bloodshed. Accordingly after they had compromised certain Emperors of sham monastic piety, and soon after overturned

the ideals of certain despotic reforming
Emperors, they were left out in the cold.
And why not, since their work was done?
After the ninth century they seldom played a
part in history. Precisely in consequence of
their victory, they became, in their dealings
with the world and the secular Church, a
conservative force. Strange to say, these
haters of the world are now the passive
defenders of public worship and morality.
When these are attacked, their fanaticism
awakes, and it is here that monasticism knows
itself to be at one with the spirit of the masses.
In other respects the regulars and the seculars
march side by side—or rather, when the
former hold out a hand to the other, they place
themselves unconditionally at the disposal
of the State. The monk-bishop, as in the
Byzantine Empire, so in the Turkish, has in
many cases not yet ceased to be a policeman
or perhaps a tax-gatherer—though a gradual
improvement is unmistakable. Along with
the State he exploits the Christian people ; he

enjoys the honours of a high official, but takes his share also in the official's corruption and incalculable changes of fortune. Thus the exaltation of the ideal found its punishment. Men tried by faith to remove all natural restrictions ; in their presumption they thought also they could dispense with the benefits of moral achievement ; and, with broken wing, they fell to the ground. A Church that had become political and secular, a monasticism of barren asceticism without a history, stubbornly maintaining national and ecclesiastical failings, was the result. The Greek Church contrived to unite in herself the opposite poles of asceticism and of the performance of ecclesiastical worship. Her proper domain, that of regulating the morals of daily life by faith, falls outside her direct cognisance. It is given over to the State and to the people— for it is essentially worldly. Nor did they find it hard gradually to annex the whole Church and to fashion it into an instrument for the attainment of their aims.

Just because the *ideal* of monasticism
and of the secular Church remained victorious in the contest with the Empire
during the eighth and ninth centuries—
just because of this did monk and priest
become *effectively* and *definitively* the slaves
of the State. In their flight from the sensuous the State overtook them ; it imposed
on them its own view of morality, but it appro-
priated their worship. Thus the Byzantine
State still shows itself the genuine though
degenerate descendant of the ancient one. But
this one end was attained that, where the
State set up expressly Christian ideas as the
standard in public law and life, it took them
in monkish form. The Byzantine code of
laws—our own social and moral views, too,
have not yet emancipated themselves from
its bonds—is in part a strange congeries of
pitiless Roman craft and of the monastic view
of the world.

Such is the history of monasticism in the
East. We must again and again remind our-

selves that to-day as of old it is the complement of the secular Church ; that even to-day
it rescues individuals from the trammels of
common life ; that there are many saints
within its borders ; that it is a protest against
barren ecclesiasticism. But this review shows
us that among the various human ideals as
based on the Gospel, the ideal of contemplation
and renunciation as a means of saving the
soul can *not* be the last and highest ; it shows
that a merely *passive* courage must at length
succumb ; and that the world will intrude
its ideals into the Church if the Christian
strives to realise his own outside of the world.
True enough is it that there are times when the
weight of injustice pressing on the active man
becomes unendurable, and that there will ever
be individuals so highly strung that they must
carry their best into solitude in order to
preserve it ; but where a *pis aller* is proclaimed as the highest virtue, there high
virtues will lose their value, and finally men
lose the reward for which those possessions

were sacrificed. Have we not in our own times seen a personality like that of Tolstoï arise from the bosom of the Russian Church— a layman, it is true, but in his writings a genuine Greek monk, to whom the only chance of Church reform lies in a radical breach with culture and history, and to whom the whole moral code—even marriage—seems defiled so far as it stands in dependence upon sense? What a terrible foe of the Greek Church Manichæism must have been of old, we can learn to calculate from the writings of this extraordinary man. The more serious the Christianity of the Greek monk, the more helpless is he before the gloomy view that the whole world lieth in the Evil One. In the long run the monk must again flee to Church authority, lest he fall a slave to Manichæism.

V.

How utterly different has been the evolution
of monasticism in the West! A glance at
its history in that region is sufficient at once
to reveal the essential differences. In the
first place, monasticism there *had* a real history; and in the second, monasticism there
made history, secular and religious alike. It
stands not merely alongside the Church,
wasting itself in silent asceticism and mystical
speculation; it stands in the very midst of
the Church—nay, it has been, next to the
Papacy, the strongest influence in all domains
of Latin Christianity. The history of Oriental
monasticism, from the fourth century to the
present day, is bound up with but few names.
Seldom did it produce sharply-marked
individualities. But the history of Western
monasticism is a history of persons and
characters.

Roman Catholicism shows us in its development a continuous chain of living reforms; and

every one of these reforms is dependent upon a new step in the development of monasticism. The foundation of the Benedictine Order in the sixth century, the Clunian Reform of the eleventh, the appearance of the Mendicant Orders in the thirteenth, the foundation of the Society of Jesus in the sixteenth, are the four great landmarks in the history of Western monasticism; but they are at the same time landmarks in the history of Western Catholicism. It was always the monks who saved the Church when sinking, emancipated her when becoming enslaved to the world, defended her when assailed. These it was that kindled hearts that were growing cold, bridled refractory spirits, recovered for the Church alienated nations. These indications alone show that in Western monasticism we have to recognise a factor of the first importance in Church and civilisation. How did it become so?

Comparatively late and slow was the advance of monasticism from East to West, for neither the natural conditions nor the civilisation of

E

the West were favourable to it. Whereas, by the middle of the fourth century, it had already spread wide in the East, and, as we may assume, arose in many districts independently of Egyptian influences, in the West it was only at the end of that century that it took firm root—nay, it was literally imported from the East. In the West its first admirers were those theologians who, like Rufinus and Jerome, had travelled over Egypt and Syria, and stood in the closest connection with the 'Greeks.' If monasteries arose, as they did, especially in Southern Gaul, it was under Eastern influences that they did so. And in the West, monasticism had from the very beginning to meet decided opposition from the Church ; whereas in the East we hear but little of such opposition. We should read the works of Sulpicius Severus (circ. 400) in order to learn what attacks monasticism in Gaul and Spain had about that time to meet before it could establish itself. The secularised Bishops, indeed, were not far from treating the monks as

Manichæans. Nevertheless, the opposition speedily abated ; even in the West it was not long before the prevailing feeling met monasticism half way, and shortly the once-anathematised name of that honest saint, Martin of Tours, came into high repute. Even before the great Augustine had espoused the cause, it had naturalised itself ; and during the storms of the great migrations, it took firm root. The monastic ideal was at first identical in its essentials both in the East and in the West, and it remained so during a thousand years—absorption in God and stern asceticism, but especially virginity, which, in West as in East, ranked as the first condition of a consecrated life. To many, indeed, virginity was neither more nor less than the very essence of Christian morality. The Egyptian anchorites, even in the West, were reckoned at all times as the fathers and models of the true Christian life. In spite of all attempts in that direction, their achievements were never cast into the shade by those of St Martin ; and the narratives of their lives, during many generations, carried on an unobtrusive mission in Italy, Gaul, and Germany—nay, even beyond the Channel, in England and the Emerald Isle. And yet, in the fifth century, the influences were already working which were to give to Western monasticism a quite other importance and a *history*. We need only remark, in passing, that the climatic conditions of the West, apart from all others, necessarily demanded a somewhat different mode of life from that of the East. " Edacitas in Graecis gula est, in Gallis natura," observed one of the earliest patrons of the Western monks. But apart from this, the internal evolution of Western Christendom, so early as the time of Tertullian, had taken a course different from that which it took in the East. Not only did practical religious questions—such as those of Penance, the Forgiveness of Sins, the Nature of the Church— come to the front, but the ancient expectations of the reign of Christ on earth were more

slowly sacrificed to the nebulous theological
speculations of the East. In such speculations
men took only a languid interest. In the so-
called 'Chiliast' conceptions the Western
Church retained a keen eye for that which the
Church of Christ ought to be ; and these conceptions were necessarily the more valuable in
proportion as, in contradistinction to Montanism, the fantastic element was stripped off,
and as the idea of a literal fulfilment of the
prophecies fell, of its own accord, into the
background. Western monasticism, in contrast to the Eastern, maintained the
Apocalyptic element of Chiliasm, which, it is
true, lay dormant for long periods, but at
critical moments constantly emerged. The
ecclesiastical ideas of Western Christendom
were fused together to a new Christian
philosophy of the world and of life by St
Augustine. Augustine's central conceptions
are the grace of God in the Church working
for righteousness, and the Church herself.
The Church, primarily as the congregation of

the faithful, but secondarily as a visible institution, is the kingdom of righteousness and
of the morally good—the Kingdom of God.
At the time of the fall of the old Empire of
the West, and of the rise of new half-heathen
States, he sketched the noble conception of a
future history of the Church.   Her business is
to fulfil humanity with the strength of the
good, and with true righteousness ; as the
visible manifestation of the City of God, she
has to press into her service the world-empire
and the kingdoms of the world ; she has to
guide and train the nations.   Only then does
Christianity come by its own, when it creates
a kingdom of moral excellence on earth, a
supramundane brotherhood of humanity :
only then does it come by its own, therefore,
when it *rules* ; and it only rules by the
rule of the Holy Catholic Church.   Spiritual
dominion over the world, a divine City of
Righteousness on earth, is thus a Christian
ideal, an ideal alike for individuals and for the
Church as a whole.   Not only the old Apoca-

lyptic hopes and the practical aims of the
West, but also Greek speculation, are brought
by Augustine into a marvellous interdepen-
dence ; they are indeed not to correct but to
delimit each other. Christian salvation, so to
speak, appears in double form ; it is the eternal
blissful contemplation of God both in this
world and in the next, but it is at the same
time in this world an imperial city of divine
gifts and moral powers.

These positions had a very different drift
from that of the painfully elaborated dogmas
of Greek Christianity. They assigned to the
Church an independent mission, for the State
and by its side. She was to serve God and
the world. This mission was a problem
demanding a worthy solution. The Greek
ideal is a problem only in so far as its realisation is but approximately possible ; in
itself it has but one meaning. But for
Augustine's conception every task resolved
itself at the same time into a question which
every man learnt to put only in proportion

as he himself actively worked at it. The
detail in the whole of the Christian conception,
clearly as it could be viewed in itself, revealed
its essence and received its value only in its
proper relations to other things.

How is the service of the world related to
the service of God? In what connection
with religion is morality to be placed? The
discovery was again made that there already
exists genuine good in this world ; that everything proceeding out of the hand of God is
good, and that man finds his blessedness only
in surrendering his *will* to God. In this
surrender of heart and will by faith and love,
which is alone possible by divine grace as
bestowed in the Sacraments, man becomes
justified and receives freedom and righteousness—that is, moral perfection. This perfection is indeed a very high good; but it is
not the highest. For the hope is still alive
that man, when raised to God, shall enjoy a
blessedness which eye hath not seen nor ear
heard—the blessedness of seeing God and

being like Him. But what is the relation of
this religious aim to the moral purpose of a
perfect righteousness in the *earthly* kingdom
of God? We may *assert* that the one is sub-
ordinate to the other, and yet *act* quite differently. This appears to be the case with
Augustine; and the Church in her march to
world-dominion followed him. Again and
again, as a matter of fact, in attempting to
identify herself with the kingdom of Christ,
she attached paramount importance to a zeal
for her own maintenance and dominion,
teaching the nations that they must seek and
find in *her* the highest good. In her consciousness that she possesses and can distribute
the divine grace of justification, she ceased in
principle to suffer anyone to seek his blessedness by a path of his own, in good works and
in asceticism. For the sake of the alone
sufficient grace of God, and at the same time
for the interest of the Church, she set at
naught for the Catholic Christian, so early as
the fifth century, the value of an asceticism

not sanctioned by the Church. But in this point she did not escape a certain amount of vacillation; for she never denied that the Church cannot guarantee salvation, and that in the last instance the individual will stand before his God, alone, and without her protection. To this hesitation on the question how far the individual Christian is to be left independent—a question which was inevitably to prove of decisive import for the position of monasticism in the Western Church—corresponds her uncertainty in appraising civil ordinances and all political forms. The Church is the kingdom of righteousness and love; outside her all is unrighteousness and hatred. But how does it then stand with States? Are they and their ordinances, after all, independent values, or do they become so only in subjecting themselves to the Church; or, finally, is it altogether impossible for them to become so? Has the Church to rule alongside of the State, or over and in the State by legal forms, or is she to rule by making all social contracts unnecessary? So far, these questions were not fully fathomed; but men lived in them. The history of Western Catholicism is the history of these ideas, until, by the great popes of the Middle Ages, they were realised in the world-dominion of the Church.

What was to be the attitude of monasticism to these ideas? The answer is not difficult. Either it had to make the attempt to come to terms with the Church, and, after the Greek fashion, to continue alongside of the Church the mere preparation for the Beyond; or else it must permit its asceticism to be curtailed by the higher aim, and to assist the Church in her great task, that of moulding mankind by the Gospel, and of building up the kingdom of Christ on earth in the Church. It did both. Western monasticism bore its share in the solution of the ecclesiastical problem; but inasmuch as it refused to sacrifice its original ideal of a contemplative life, its own ideals became problems; and as it helped towards realising the aims of the Church, but could not always follow in her path, it passed through peculiar vicissitudes. Let us endeavour to sketch in brief the stages of this history.

VI.

I⊤ was in Italy, in the sixth century, that monasticism took the first new stride in its development. St Benedict of Nursia gave it a new rule, and rendered it capable of organised activity and fruitful exertion. It was necessary that it should be itself re-organised before it could effectively act. Certainly, considered from the point of view of its content, the rule was in no sense new ; but there were in the West, at the beginning of the sixth century, highly varied, and in part highly doubtful, forms of monasticism. The merit of Benedict consists in the re-duction of these forms to a single one, and that the most effective. Still greater than the merit was the result. The unconditional obedience to which the monks were constrained, their organisation, the opposition to the vagrant and debased monks, the strict regulation of daily life, and the assertion of work—and in the first instance of agriculture —as a duty ; all these are notable facts. True, we have met the demand for obedience and for work in Eastern rules ; nor in the new rule is this demand yet specially recognised as of paramount importance ; but in the sequel it became of the most decisive moment. And what a change did it introduce ! From the rude, somewhat dispersed, and disordered colonies of monks, arose regular united societies, with a vast capacity for work that had to find a field for its exercise. That great occupant of the see of Peter, Gregory the First, himself a monk in head and heart, pressed into his service this new force and made it an agent of the Church. Even before this the Ostrogoth statesman Cassiodorus, in retreating into the cloister

after a long and weary life, had introduced
scientific labour into the programme of the
monastery, and himself began by compiling
historical and theological manuals for the
cloister. From the seventh century onwards
we meet brethren of the Benedictine Order
far in the West. They clear woods, they
turn deserts into ploughland, they study—
with good or bad conscience—the lays of
heathen poets and the writings of historians
or philosophers. Monasteries and monastic
schools begin to flourish; and every single
settlement is at the same time a centre of
religious life and of education in the country.
By the help of these bands the Roman
Bishop was enabled to introduce or to preserve, in the West, Christianity and a remnant of the ancient culture : by their means
he Romanised the new German states. We
say the Roman Bishop—for such activity on
the part of his Order had been no part of the
scheme of Benedict, nor did it naturally
arise out of his Rule, nor yet was it consciously

to nothing. The monasteries became ever more and more dependent, not only on the bishops, but also on the great ones of the land. The abbots tended to become more and more what they had long been in fact, mere courtiers : it was soon only certain ceremonies that distinguished the regular clergy from the secular. In the tenth century it appeared as if monasticism had well-nigh played its part in the West : it seemed—a few houses, chiefly nunneries, being disregarded—as if Western monasticism had succumbed to the danger which in the East could not possibly in this way arise—it had become worldly, and vulgarly worldly, not by a hair's breadth higher than the world at large. In the tenth century, Pope, Church, and monastery alike seemed to have reached the last stage of decrepitude.

F

VII.

AND yet there had already begun a second movement in the Church; a second revival of monasticism. This revival started in France. The monastery of Clugny, founded so early as the tenth century, became the home of that great reform of the Church which the West experienced in the eleventh. Begun by monks, it was at first supported by pious and intelligent princes and bishops as a counterpoise to the secularised Papacy; but later the great Hildebrand took it up, and alike as Cardinal and as Pope opposed it to the princes and the secularised clergy. The West gained by it an effective reformation of the Church; a reformation, however, not on Evangelical but on Catholic lines. The aims of this new movement were in the first instance a restoration of the old discipline, of true renunciation and piety in the monasteries themselves; but later, first, a subjection of the secular clergy to the regulars, and, secondly, the dominion of the whole spiritualty, as regulated by the monks, over the laity—princes and nations alike. The great reform of the monks of Clugny and of their mighty Pope presents itself first as the energetic attempt to conform the life of the whole spiritualty to monastic ordinances. In this movement Western monasticism for the first time puts forth the decisive claim to pose as the only Christian life for all adult believers, and to ensure the general recognition of this claim. Monasticism in the West must inevitably come again and again into contact with the secular Church, for the reason that it can never cease itself to put forth claims on the whole of Christendom or to serve the Church. The Christian freedom at which it aims is to it, in spite of all vacillation, not only a freedom of the individual *from* the world, but the freedom of Christendom for the service of God *in* the world. We Evangelicals can even to-day still judge this great movement with sympathy : for in it expression is given to the consciousness that within the Church there can be only one morality and only one ideal of life, and that to this therefore all adult Christians are pledged. If monasticism is really the highest form of Christianity, it comes to this, that all adult confessors should be subjected to the monastic rule, and all Christians in their nonage—*i.e.*, in the mediæval view all the laity—should be urged at least to obedience. Such were the ideas that dominated Clugny and Clugny's great Pope. Hence the stern enforcement of the celibacy of the clergy ; hence the struggle against the secularisation of the spiritualty, and specially against simony ; hence the monastic discipline of the priests. And what about his effort after political supremacy ? Though it might from this point of view be looked on as a mere *parergon* which was to last because, and only so long as, the true conversion of the world was incomplete, yet here begin the points of difference between

monasticism and the reformed secular Church.
It is possible so to represent the ideas of
Hildebrand and those of his more earnest
friends as to make them appear to differ only
by a shade. Yet this shade of difference
led to policies totally opposed. From the
very first voices were heard, even among
the most zealous supporters of the Pope,
crying that it was enough to reform manners
and to cherish piety: it was not for the
Church to rule in the style and with the
weapons of the State. These voices demanded
a true return to apostolic life, and a renewal
of the Early Church. It is incorrect to
describe these efforts of the monks as if they
betokened a retrogression to the standard
of the Greek Church, and thus fell outside
the circle of Western Catholicism. The real
truth is, these monks had a positive aim—
Christian life for the *whole* of Christendom.
But since tradition offered to them a conception of a supernaturally renewed Empire,
which they did not renounce the hope of

realising on earth, they conceived an almost invincible mistrust of the 'parergon,' which the Roman Bishop held out and for which he strove. In this mistrust was included that shrinking from everything in the Church that recalled political or legal ordinances. Repugnance to public law and to the State is in the Western monasticism as character-istic as in the East the reason is plain why Greek ascetics show no such repugnance. But in the eleventh century devotion to the Church and her ruler was powerful enough to prevent an open conflict between the reformed clergy and the monks. In the Sacrament of Penance the Church possessed the strongest means of binding even the monks to herself. With conscience stained and courage broken, many bowed to the will of the great monastic Pope. And it was precisely those that had most willingly dedicated their whole life to God whom he drew out of the quiet of the monastery. He knew well that only that monk will help to subjugate the world who shuns it and strives to free himself from it. Renunciation of the world in the service of a world-ruling Church—such is the amazing problem that Gregory solved for the next century and a half. But Gregory's aims, and those of the reformed bishops, with all their political character, were spiritual also. Only as spiritual did they transform the masses, and inflame them against the worldly clergy in upper Italy, or against simoniacal princes throughout Europe. A new religious zeal stirred the nations, and specially the Romance nations, of the West. The enthusiasm of the Crusades was the direct fruit of the monastic reform of the eleventh century. That religious revival which Europe experienced is expressed most vividly in them. The dominion of the Church is to be consummated on earth. It was the ideas of the world-ruling monk of Clugny that led the van of the Crusades; and the Crusaders brought back from the Holy Land and the Holy Places a new, or at least till now rare form of Christian piety — that of absorption in the sufferings and in the Via Dolorosa of Christ. Asceticism, once negative, received a positive form and a new positive aim, that of becoming one with the Redeemer by fervent love and perfect imitation. A personal element, working from heart to heart, began to vivify the hitherto unimpassioned and aimless struggle of self-abnegation, and to awaken the sleeping subjectivity. Even to monasticism, though as a rule only in a few isolated cases, it lent an inner impulse. The great number of new Orders that were founded at this time, specially in France, bears witness to the general enthusiasm. It was then that arose the Carthusians, the Cistercians, the Præmonstratensians, the Carmelites, and many other Orders. But the constant appearance of fresh Orders only shows that monasticism, in alliance with the secular Church, was ever losing its special character. Each new Order sought to call back the monks to their old

austerity and to drag them away from
secularisation; but in the very act of subjecting itself to the secular Church, it was
annexed and exploited by the Church. It
shows the illusions in which men moved
that the Orders which were founded to restore
the original monasticism, by the very terms of
their foundation expressly announced their
subjection to the bishops, and thenceforward
renounced not only the care of souls, but all
special programmes within the Church and
for the Church. In the twelfth century the
dependence of Christendom, and thus also
of monasticism, on the Church is still a very
naïve one: the contradiction between the
actual form of the world-ruling Church and
the Gospel which she preaches is felt indeed
but always suppressed, and criticism of the
claims and of the constitution of the Church
is as yet ineffective. We need only mention
the name of a single man, that of Bernard
of Clairvaux, in order to see as in a picture
alike all the greatness which this second

monastic reform of the Church introduced, and its limitations and illusions. The same monk who in the quiet of his cell speaks a new language of devotion, who dedicates his soul entirely to the Bridegroom, who urges Christendom to forsake the world, who tells the Pope that he is called to the chair of Peter not for dominion but for service : this same man was yet imbued with all the hierarchical prejudices of his time, and himself led the politics of the world-ruling Church. But it was precisely because monasticism in that age went with the Church that it was able to do so great a work for her. It roused, it is true, a reform in the Church ; but this reform, in the long run, came to strengthen the political power of the Church, and so to increase her secularisation—a strange and yet easily intelligible result. The domain in which Church and cloister found constantly their common ground was the contest with all the claims of the laity, and specially of the princes, on the Church.

Western monasticism took this to be a
'liberation from the world,' and therefore
offered its services in the struggle to the
Church. Only by observing this can we
understand how one and the same man
in that age could be at once an upright
monk and a prince of the Church, or how
he could deceive himself and others, or even
be uncertain, as to the final aims of this
opposition to the State.

VIII.

A NEW age arose, with which the old conceptions did not harmonise. The Church
had attained to political world-dominion;
she had either actually overcome, or was on
the point of overcoming, the Empire and the
old State order. The aims and results of the
mighty efforts put forth by the Church in the
eleventh and twelfth centuries had now been
made manifest; but now a movement began

among the laity and in the nations to emancipate themselves from the tutelage of the
hierarchy. In social movements, in religious
sectarianism, in pious unions which failed to
find satisfaction in official piety, in the en-
deavours of nations and princes to order their
own concerns independently, was heralded
the approach of a new era. For a whole
century the secular Church succeeded in
holding back the tide; and in doing so she
was aided by a fresh phenomenon in monasticism which is marked by the foundation
of the mendicant Orders.

The figure of the tenderest and most
loveable of all monks, the quaint saint of
Assisi, stands out brilliantly in the history
of the Middle Ages. Here, however, we are
not asking what was his character, but what
were his aims in devoting himself to the
service of God and of his brethren. In the
first place he desired to renew the life of the
Apostles by imitating the poverty of their
life and their preaching of the Gospel. This

preaching was to arouse penitence in Christendom and to make Christendom effectively
that which she already was through her possession of the Holy Sacraments. A society
of brethren was to be formed which, like the
Apostles, should possess nothing but penitence, faith, and love, and which should own
no other aim than to serve others and to win
souls. St Francis never clearly defined how
far this society was to extend itself. He
was no politician, and never intruded on the
domain of government. But what could
converts, made by the preaching of the poor
brethren, have become, but themselves brethren, serving itinerant preachers, in their turn ?
For them St Francis himself laid down fixed
and settled rules. Neither individuals nor
even the society, united as it was for a
truly Christ-like life, was to possess property
of any kind. " Go sell all that thou hast."
Life in God, suffering along with His Son, love
for His creatures, human and other, service
even to the sacrifice of one's own life, the

riches of the soul, which possesses nothing but
the Saviour—such was the Gospel of St Francis.
If any man ever realised in his life what he
preached, St Francis was that man.   And—
what is the characteristic mark of this Western movement—intense as this asceticism
was, heartfelt as this religion was, it did
not drive its disciples into solitude or the
desert, but the reverse.   Christendom, nay,
the whole world, was to be won for this
new and yet old Christianity of repentance,
renunciation, and love.   A Christian world—
this conception, at the beginning of the
thirteenth century, had a quite other content
than in the sixth and eleventh ; not only
because the geographical horizon had extended itself for the West, but to a higher
degree because the poor and the ordinary
man were now to be reckoned as part of that
world.   Western monasticism, down to the
end of the twelfth century, had been essentially
an aristocratic institution ; the privileges of
the monasteries were in most cases conditioned

by the descent of their inmates. The monastic schools were as a rule open only to the nobility. To the coarse and common people the monastery remained as inaccessible as the castle. There were no popular Orders and few popular monks. St Francis did not break down the walls of the noble monasteries but raised alongside them huts for poor and rich. He thus restored the Gospel to the people, who had hitherto possessed only the priest and the Sacrament. But the saint of Assisi was the most submissive son of the Church and of the Pope in history. His labours were devoted to the service of the Church. Thus he was the first to give to monasticism—for a monasticism his brotherhood became, little as he meant it—special tasks for Christianity as a whole, but in the bosom of the Church : for care for the Church is care for salvation. Clugny and its monks had exclusively devoted themselves to the reform of the spiritualty. St Francis would know no distinctions. We may say without

exaggeration that he wished not to found a
new order of monks but to revolutionise the
world—to make the world a fair garden,
colonised by men who follow Christ, who
need nothing, in whose hearts is God. It
was love that enlarged his horizon : his fancy
neither grew rankly luxuriant, nor did it
become barren through his stern asceticism :
his determination to serve Church and Christianity remained to the end strong and
powerful, though he was constrained with
pain to see how the Church corrected and
narrowed his creation. Hundreds of thousands
flocked to him. But what were thousands
when it was a question of millions ? The
emergence of the so-called Tertiary Brethren
by the side of the strict monastic order is
on one side, of course, an indication that this
Gospel does not penetrate into human society
without compromise, but on the other a
shining example of the far-reaching influence
of the Franciscan preaching. The Tertiaries
kept up their secular callings, their marriages

and their possessions; but they adapted
themselves as far as possible to the monastic
life, held themselves aloof from public affairs,
and devoted themselves, as far as they could,
to asceticism and works of piety. This institution, which formed itself without any
recognised founder, is a striking proof of the
universal character of the Franciscan movement. Sects had led the way; but the
brotherhood remained true to the Church.
Nay, the interest of the laity in the life and
in the sacraments of *the Church* was awakened
by them; through them the idea grew slowly
effective that a layman, sincerely obedient
to the Church and inwardly pious, has a right
to share in the highest good which the Church
can communicate. The conception of a
double morality differing in value, could on
this basis be transformed into another more
tolerable conception of a morality differing
only in kind. An *active* Christian life may
be of equal value with the contemplative; the
latter is only a more direct path to salvation.

G

A newly moulded piety, dominated by the surrender of the soul to Christ, spread forth from Assisi and made itself master of the Church. It was religious individuality and freedom that had been awakened ; Christianity as the *religion* of poverty and love was to come by its own as opposed to the degeneracy in morality and politics.

The finest of mediæval hymns, the mightiest of mediæval sermons, belong to the Franciscan Order or to the nearly-related Dominicans. But to art and science also these Orders gave a new impulse. All the important schoolmen of the thirteenth century — a Thomas Aquinas, a Bonaventura, an Albertus Magnus— were mendicant monks. The noblest paintings of the old Italian school are inspired by the new spirit, the spirit of absorption in the sufferings of Christ, of a holy sorrow and a transcendental strength. A Dante, a Giotto, and again a Tauler, and a Berthold of Ratisbon—all these, in their feelings, thoughts, and creations, lived in the

religious ideas of the mendicant Orders. But—
what is more significant—these monks stooped
to the populace and to individuals. They
had an eye for their sorrows and an ear for
their complaints. They lived with the
people, they preached to the people in their
own language, and they brought them a
consolation they could understand. What
the sacrament and the services had hitherto
failed to give—a certainty of salvation—
the mysticism of the Orders aimed at pro-
ducing: but not outside of the Church means
of grace. The eye must learn to see the
Saviour; the soul must attain peace by
sensuous perception of His presence. But the
'theology,' which here arose, proclaimed also
the religious freedom and blessedness of souls
lifted above the world and conscious of their
God. If by this idea it did not actually
begin the Evangelical Reformation, it made
the path straight for it.

By the help of the mendicant Orders, of
which she availed herself to the full, the

Church was able in the thirteenth century
to maintain herself at the height of her
dominion. She won back the hearts of the
faithful; but at the same time, through
the activity of the monks, she ordered and
brought to perfection her hold on the goods
of the world, science, art, and law. It was
then that the body of canon law was completed, which regulates all the relations of
life from the standpoint of the Church's
world-dominion, and of an asceticism devoted
to her service. This canon law is no longer
recognised in civilised states, but its ideas
still bear fruit. To a much higher degree
are philosophy and theology, as well as social
politics, still dependent on the mode of
thought which in the thirteenth century, in
the mendicant Orders, led to the masterly
development of great scholastic systems.
Through these Orders, again, the Church succeeded in overcoming the sectarian movements
that had taken hold of the laity. It was the
mendicants who with furious zeal conquered

the heretical, but, alas! also free-spirited and
evangelical, movements of the thirteenth
century. Thus here also they made common
cause with the world-ruling Church, the
Church of politics and of the sword: nay,
they became precisely the most favoured
clerical servants of the Popes, who endowed
them with the highest privileges, and per-
mitted them everywhere to interfere with the
regular administration of the Church and with
the cure of souls. In the mendicant Orders,
the Roman Pope found a tool wherewith to
weld the national churches of the country
more closely to his see, and to crush the
independence of the Bishops. Thus they had
the largest share in the Romanising of the
Catholic Church in Europe, and also influenced in many ways the older foundations
which sprang out of the Benedictine Rule.
But they became secularised as speedily as
any other Order before them. The connection
with the secular Church proved once again
fatal to monasticism. That connection had

been from the first extraordinarily close— Francis had been compelled to yield as if to a decree of Fate—and the ruin was all the more rapid. What was meant to raise them above the world—their poverty—proved but an occasion of specific secularisation to those who no longer took poverty seriously. They saw themselves led to speculate on the coarseness, the superstition, and the sluggishness of the masses ; and they became, like the masses, coarse, superstitious, and sluggish.

Yet the high ideal set before Christendom by St Francis could not disappear without shaking to their foundations the Church and the Order founded by him. When one party in the Order urged a modification of the strictness of the regulations imposing poverty, another, faithful to the Master, arose to defend them. When the Popes took up the cause of the former, the zealous party turned their criticism upon the Papacy and the secular Church. Complaints of the corruption of the Church had long been uttered by individual monks,

but they had always died away again. The
strife of the Church against the states
and their claims had hitherto constantly
enticed monasticism to recognise in the programme of the Church the beginning of the
realisation of its own. But now arose the
idea which had always lain dormant in
monasticism and had again and again been
suppressed. The tie with Church and Papacy
was sundered: ancient apocalyptic ideas
emerged; the Papal Church appeared as
Babylon, as the Kingdom of Antichrist, who
has falsified the true Christianity of renunciation and poverty. The whole history of
the Church appeared suddenly in the light of
a monstrous apostasy; and the Pope no longer
as the successor of Peter but as the heir of
Constantine. It was hopeless to attempt to
move the Church to turn back. Nothing but
a new revelation of the Spirit could avail to
save her, and men accordingly looked for a
future final Gospel of Christian perfection.
With all the means in her power the Church

suppressed this dangerous uprising. She pronounced the teachings of the Franciscans on the poverty of Christ and the Apostles to be heresy, and she demanded submission. A bitter struggle was the result. Christendom witnessed the new spectacle of the secular Church in arms against a doctrine of renunciation that had become aggressive. With the courage of men who had sacrificed all, the Spirituals preached to Pope and Bishop their doctrine of poverty, and sealed their testimony at the stake. At the end of the fourteenth century the secular Church came forth, victorious and unchanged, from her strife with poverty. Thus once again, at the end of the Middle Ages, the sleeping but ever reviving antagonism between the aims of the Church and the aims of monasticism had come to light in a terrible crisis. But monasticism was vanquished. The foundation of the mendicant Orders was its last great attempt in the Middle Ages to assert itself and its ideal in the Church as a

whole while maintaining its connection with
the history and constitution of that Church.
But the development of the Franciscan
Order was twofold. The one party, from
the very first, resigned its original ideal,
subjected itself completely to the Church,
and became speedily secularised ; the other
sought to maintain its ideal, made that ideal
stricter, set it up even against the Church,
and exhausted itself, until it succumbed, in
fantastic pursuits. This development will to
some appear an unredeemed tragedy ; but it
will perhaps not seem an unmixed evil to
those who recognise that individuals of the
Order which strove to emancipate itself from
the Church, sought deliverance at the hands
of the State, and, in opposition to the claims
of the Church, which they no longer or only
partially admitted, began to defend the
independence and ordinances of the State.
It was the Franciscans who, in the fourteenth
century, discovered a scientific foundation for
the Hohenstaufen theory of politics. Western

monasticism, as we learn from this astonishing volte-face, is unable to exist for any length of time without a close alliance with the forces of society. When the Church is not available, it seeks even the State. Yet this movement was but transitory. In the fifteenth century a deathly stillness reigns in the Order, which is now in entire subjection to the Church; attempts at reform were feeble, and resulted in no fresh life. In the age of the Renascence monasticism — with a few honourable exceptions—seemed to have condemned itself to inaction and uselessness. Yet the new culture, whose supporters, it is true, frequently spent their shafts of ridicule on the ignorant, slavish, and hypocritical monks, was not utterly hostile to ascetic ideals. Rather did the vision reappear of a wise and pious man, absorbed in the enjoyment of a quiet contemplation of heaven, without neglecting the world, in peaceful detachment from the noises of the day; who needs nothing because in spirit he possesses all. The attempt was even

made to revive this ideal in the traditional
forms of cloister-life; nor did it everywhere
fail. But it was only given to isolated
individuals to unite the rule of the convent
with the study of Cicero or Plato, and to be
sufficient for both. The scholar who was at
the same time a man of the world, and who
at his desk became enthusiastic for Stoical
indifference or for Franciscan independence
of externals, was anything but a monk; and
the Church, in spite of all classical and
edifying dissertations, remained as she was.
The poor, as in the days before St Francis
had shown them the way, sought to secure
their salvation in pious and enthusiastic
unions of every kind, which were, it is true,
of occasional service to the Church, but nevertheless were to her a constant danger.

IX.

WHAT was left? What new form of monasticism remained possible after all these

attempts? None—or rather, perhaps, one, which in truth is no longer one, and yet became the last and in a true sense the authentic word of Western monasticism. It remained possible to begin with reversing the relations between asceticism and ecclesiastical service; to keep at once in the eye, as the purposed and highest aim, the ideal which had always floated before the gaze of Western monasticism, but had never been taken up save with hesitation. It remained possible to find, instead of an ascetic union with ecclesiastical tendencies, a society that should pursue no other aim than to strengthen and extend the dominion of the Church. The glory of recognising this possibility, and of understanding the lessons of history, belongs to the Spaniard, Ignatius Loyola. His creation, the Society of Jesus, which he set up against the Reformation, is no monasticism in the oldest sense of the word, nay, it appears as a downright protest against the monasticism of a St Antony or a St Francis. True,

the Society is equipped with all the rules of
the older Orders; but its first principle is
that which they had uncertainly viewed as a
side-purpose, or which they had unwillingly
allowed to be imposed upon them by circumstances. To the Jesuits all asceticism, all
renunciation, is but a means to an end. Emancipation from the world extends only so far as
such emancipation helps towards domination
over the world—a domination exercised *politi-
cally* by means of the Church. The professed
aim of the Order is the dominion of the Church
over the world. Religious enthusiasm, culture and barbarism, splendour and squalor,
diplomacy and simplicity, all alike are em-
ployed by this Order to attain the one
purpose to which it has dedicated itself. In
it, Western Catholicism, so to speak, neu-
tralised monasticism, and gave it a turn by
which it made the aims of monasticism its
own. And yet the Society was not the
work of a cunning, calculating intelligence
merely. As it arose, it was the product of

a high enthusiasm, but of an enthusiasm from within that Church which had already rejected any sort of evangelical reform, and which had resolved to maintain itself for ever in the form given to it, in the course of a long history, by worldly wisdom and policy.

On the other side, the Jesuit Order is the last and authentic word of Western monasticism.   Its rise, no less than its nature, lies entirely on the lines which we have traced from Benedict to Bernard, and from Bernard to the mendicants.   The Society of Jesus has solved the problems to which they were unequal, and has attained the objects for which they strove.   It produced a new form of piety, and gave to that piety a special expression and a methodical form, and in this respect it made a successful appeal to the whole of Catholic Christianity.   It has known how to interest the laity in the Church, and has opened to them in its mysticism that which hitherto had been denied to them. It has penetrated the life of the Church in all its domains, and brought the faithful to the feet of the Pope. But not only has the Order constantly pursued objects of its own in the service of the Church; it has also known how to maintain itself at all times in a certain independence of her. While it has not seldom corrected the policy of the Popes in accordance with the programme of the Papacy, it to-day rules the Church by its peculiar Christianity, its fantastic and sensuous mode of worship, and its political morality. It never became a mere tool in the hand of the Church, and it never, like the earlier Orders, sank into mere insignificance. It never transformed itself into a department of the Church; rather did the Church fall under the domination of the Jesuits. In the Society of Jesus, in fact, monasticism has actually won the victory over the secular Church of the West.

Monasticism, then, prevailed; but what form of monasticism? Not that of St Francis; but one which had previously made the programme of the Church its own, and thus emptied and renounced its own essence. In it asceticism and renunciation have become mere political forms and instruments; diplomacy and a sensuous mysticism have taken the place of a simple piety and moral discipline. This monasticism can no longer materially maintain its genuineness except by its opposition to states and their culture, and by making small account of the individual. Under the supremacy of the Jesuits the Church has become specifically and definitively secularised; she opposes to the world, to history, and to civilisation, *her own* worldly possessions, which are the legacy of the Middle Ages. Her consciousness of 'other-worldliness' she strengthens to-day mainly by her opposition to the culture of the Renascence and of the Reformation; but she draws her strength from the failings and defects of that culture and from the mistakes of its protectors. If we regard the negative attitude of the Church to the modern State as the expression of her

' other-worldly ' sentiment, then monasticism has indeed conquered in her; but if we see, in the manner in which she to-day maintains this attitude, an essential secularisation, then it is precisely the Jesuitic monasticism which is to be made answerable therefor. As historical factors, the other Orders are to-day nearly without importance. The Society of Jesus influenced the older and the younger almost without exception. Whether they returned, like the Trappists, to an Oriental silence, or whether some of them, in the style of the old Egyptian monks, have come to view even ecclesiastical learning with mistrust, and to declaim against it; whether they continue their existence divided between the world and asceticism, though it be to the attainment of something notable in social usefulness or in the salvation of individuals—in any case they have ceased to be an historical factor. Their place has been taken by the Jesuits, and by the ' Congregations,' those elastic and pliant creations in which the

H

spirit of the Jesuitic Order has found a point of contact with the needs and institutions of modern society. The Congregations, directed in the spirit of the Society of Jesus, and the innumerable 'free' Catholic associations which work in the same spirit, and which are at need secular or spiritual, free or 'tied'; these are the real Catholic monasticism of modern times.

In the Church of the West, which set before herself moral and political aims, monasticism in its original form, and the ideals of that monasticism, have had in the long run but sporadic effects. So far as it decided to bear its part in the secular mission of the Church, it had to transform itself into that society which betokens its freedom from the world by a worldly and political reaction against culture and history, and which thus brought to completion the secularisation of the Church. Monasticism in the East maintained its independence at the cost of stagnation; monasticism in the West remained effectual at the cost of losing its essential principle. In the East it was shattered, because it thought it could despise moral effort for the benefit of the world; and in the West it succumbed, because it subjected itself to a Church that devoted religion and morality to the service of politics. But there, as here, it was the Church herself that engendered monasticism and appointed its ideals; and thus in East and West alike, though after long vacillation and severe struggles, monasticism came finally to be the protector of ecclesiastical tradition and the guardian of ecclesiastical empiricism; and so its original aims were transformed into their opposites.

Even to-day, to certain hearts weary of the world, monasticism may indeed bring peace; but the view of history passes beyond monasticism to the message of Luther, that man begins the imitation of Christ when, in his calling and in his sphere of life, he aids in the work of God's kingdom by faith and ministering love. Even this ideal is not simply identical with the content of the Gospel message; but it points out the lines along which the Christian must move, and secures him against insincerity and self-deception. Like all ideals, it was set up when men were striving to escape from an intolerable position; and, like them, it was soon falsified and tainted by the world. But if it aims to be no more than the confession that no man attains to the perfection of life which is set before us in the Gospel; and if it expresses the fact that in any condition the Christian may rely on the divine help and grace; then it will be the strength of the weak, and in the strife of creeds it may yet be a signal of peace.

The

Confessions of St Augustine

The

Confessions of St Augustine

DURING the period between the death of
Constantine and the sack of Rome by the
Vandals, that is, from about 340 A.D. to 450,
took place the accumulation of the spiritual
capital inherited from antiquity by the Middle
Ages. Whether we look at religion and
theology, or at science and politics, or at the
leading ideas generally of the mediæval mind,
everywhere we become conscious of the
absolute dependence of these ideas on the
intellectual acquisitions made by the Fathers
of the Church in the century of migrations.
These acquisitions, it is true, do not themselves bear the stamp of new production;
rather are they entirely a selection from a

much richer abundance of ideas and living forces.

When, in the reign of Constantine, the Church had gained the victory, her leaders sought to make themselves masters of all forms of spiritual life, and to subject everybody and everything to the dominion of the Church and her spirit. The great task, long since commenced, of fusing Christianity with the Empire and with ancient culture, was finished with astonishing quickness. Now first was the union between the Christian religion and ancient philosophy completed. Through the favour of circumstances an active interchange between East and West, Rome and Greece, was again brought about. The Latin Church was equipped with a store of Greek philosophy immediately before the great severance between East and West. It would almost seem that the impending doom, the approaching night of barbarism, had been already foreboded. The firm building of the Church was completed in haste. Whatever

in Greek philosophy seemed capable of use
was drawn into the scheme of dogmatic teaching ; the remainder was relegated to the rear
as dangerous or as heretical, and thus
gradually got rid of. The constitution of the
Church was supplemented from the tried forms
of the imperial constitution ; the ecclesiastical
canons followed the lines of Roman law.
Public service was revised and its forms
extended. Already whatever appeared imposing and venerable in the old heathen
mysteries had been long imitated ; but now the
whole service became still more magnificent.
Thus was formed that splendid pomp, that
wonderful union of elevated thoughts with
ceremonial forms, which even to-day makes
the Catholic service so impressive. Art, again,
was not forgotten : ancient tradition was
made to yield up certain of its 'motives'—
few, but those highly significant and of high
creative import—to which the Church lent
the glamour of sanctity. Even the stores of
ancient culture, and the literature of leisure,

were prepared for the good of the coming centuries. The old heathen fables, heroic sagas, and novels were sifted and transformed into Christian Lives of Saints.

In every case the ascetic ideal of the Church formed the basis of these stories; though the contrast to the varied and sinful life in which this ideal was given its play, lent an especial charm to the old legends in their new form.

Thus everything borrowed from antiquity was made 'Christian,' and received, by its union with sanctity, the guarantee of permanence. The remnant of old culture, thus incorporated with the Church, was now able to defy the approaching storms and to serve the coming nations.

But it was after all a mere remnant, a poor selection from the capital of a falling world, protected by the authority of sanctity; not, indeed, lacking in inner unity, but as yet without progressive force or the power of growth.

In the Middle Ages, during more than seven centuries, if we disregard the fresh and youthful vigour contributed by the Germanic races, the West remained confined to the above possession; but, on the other hand, it owned a treasure of incomparable fulness, a man who lived at the end of the ancient time, and who projected his life over the centuries of the new—Augustine.

Between St Paul the Apostle and Luther the Reformer, the Christian Church has possessed no one who could measure himself with Augustine; and in comprehensive influence no other is to be compared with him. We are right, both in the Middle Ages and to-day, to mark a distinction between the spirit of the East and that of the West; and we are right to observe in the latter a life and motion, the straining of mighty forces, high problems, and great aims. But, if so, the *Church* of the West at least owes this peculiarity of hers in no small degree to one man, Augustine. Along with the Church he served, he has moved through the centuries. We find him in the great mediæval theologians, including the greatest, Thomas Aquinas. His spirit sways the pietists and mystics of those ages : St Bernard no less than Thomas à Kempis. It is he that inspires the ecclesiastical reformers—those of the Karling epoch as much as a Wyclif, a Hus, a Wesel and a Wessel : while, on the other hand, it is the same man that gives to the ambitious Popes the ideal of a theocratic state to be realised on earth.

All this, perhaps, may to us, to-day, seem somewhat foreign : our culture, it is said, springs from the Renascence and the Reformation. True enough ; but the spirit of Augustine ruled the beginnings of both. Upon Augustine, Petrarch and the great masters of the Renascence formed themselves ; and without him Luther is not to be understood. Augustine, the founder of Roman Catholicism, is at the same time the only Father of the Church from whom Luther received any effective teaching, or whom the humanists honoured as a hero.

But Augustine has still closer points of contact with us than these. The religious language we speak, so familiar to us from songs, prayers, and books of devotion, bears the stamp of his mind. We speak, without knowing it, in his words; and it was he who first taught the deepest emotions how to find expression, and lent words to the eloquence of the heart. I am not here speaking of what is called the tongue of Zion. In this also he has his share, though to but a small degree. But it is the language of simple piety and of powerful Christian pathos; and further, that of our psychologists and pedagogues is still under his influence. Hundreds of great masters have since his time been given us; they have guided our thoughts, warmed our emotions, enriched our speech; but none has supplanted Augustine.

Finally, which is the main point, we find in his delineation of the essence of religion and of the deepest problems of morality, such striking depth and truth of observation, that we must still honour him as our master, and that his memory is still able in some measure, even to-day, to unite Protestant and Catholic.

I do not propose to set before you a complete picture of the activity and influence of this man. I prefer rather to portray him merely according to the work in which he has portrayed himself — the 'Confessions' — the most characteristic of the many writings he has left us.

This work Augustine wrote in mature years —he was then forty-six—and twelve years after his baptism at Milan. He had already been for some time Bishop of Hippo in Northern Africa, when he felt impelled to give to himself and to the world, in the form of a confession to God, an account of his life down to his baptism, in order that, as he says, God might be praised. "He hath made us, but we had brought ourselves to destruction ; He who made us, also hath made us anew." " I tell this to the whole race of man, howsoever few thereof may read my writing, in order that I and all who read this may think from how great a depth must man cry to God." At the end of his life, thirty years later, he looked back to this work. He calls it the one of his books which is read most fondly and most often. Some points in it, it is true, he himself censures ; but, as a whole, in the presence of death itself, he marks it as a witness of the truth. It was not to be a mingling of Dichtung and Wahrheit ; but he meant, plainly and without reserve, to show in the book what he had been.

The significance of the ' Confessions' is as great on the side of form as on that of content. Before all, they were a literary *achievement*. No poet, no philosopher before him undertook what he here performed ; and I may add that almost a thousand years had to pass before a similar thing was done. It was the poets of the Renascence, who formed themselves on Augustine, that first gained from his example the daring to depict themselves and to present their personality to the world. For what do the 'Confessions' of Augustine contain? The portrait of a soul—not psychological disquisitions on the Understanding, the Will, and the Emotions in Man, not abstract investigations into the nature of the soul, not superficial reasonings and moralising introspections like the Meditations of Marcus Aurelius, but the most exact portraiture of a distinct human personality, in his development from childhood to full age, with all his propensities, feelings, aims, mistakes ; a portrait of a soul, in fact, drawn with a perfection of observation that leaves on one side the mechanical devices of psychology, and pursues the method of the physician and the physiologist.

Observation, indeed, is the strong point of Augustine. Because he observes, he is interested in everything that the professed philosopher disregards. He depicts the infant in the cradle and the naughtinesses of

the child; and he passes reflections on the
'innocence of childhood.' He watches the
beginnings of speech, and shows how speech
develops itself slowly out of the mimetic
tendency. He stands by the games of
children, and sees in the child the adult, in
the adult the child. Full of sympathy, he
listens to the first sighs of the boy who has to
learn. He accompanies him as he leaves
home for school, and is thus plunged into the
stream of human society. He observes the
dominant educational system, how it reposes on
fear and ambition. He compassionates youth
on the false and fruitless matter that it has
to learn. He is of opinion that we ought
only to learn what is true, and that grammar
is better than mythology, physics better than
windy speculation. Next, he watches the
busy doings of the adult : " The antics of
children are called business in the grown-up."
He appraises society, and finds that every
man in it strives to obtain good things, and
that malice is an aim in itself to no man ; but

I

he finds, on the other hand, that the man who does not set his heart on moral perfection, sinks step by step to lower ideals, and that we have a greater repugnance to the good and holy, the longer we live without goodness and holiness. He observes the fascination and contagious power of social evils : "O Friendship, worse than the deepest enmity, unfathomable betrayer of souls ! Merely because someone says, 'Come, let us do this or that,' and we are ashamed not to be shameless." He reveals the dependence of the individual on the opinion of others : "Each man thinks he pushes others, and is only pushed in the deeper himself." He regards the individual altogether not as a free, self-guiding personality, but as a link in an endless chain : "We wear the fetters of our mortality, and are fettered to society." He watches the contented beggar, and indulges in reflections ; he gives an amusing picture of the repute and the hollowness of a renowned teacher. He paints for us the professors and the students ;

the busy, trifling, charming intercourse between friends following the same calling. What is *characteristic*, indeed, never escapes him. But, above all, he watches the most secret motions of his own heart; he tracks the dainty ripples and mighty upheavings of his own feelings. He knows every subterfuge and by-path by which man strives to escape from his God and his high destiny.

If we consider what was written elsewhere at that time, and the manner in which it was written, we are struck dumb with astonishment at the sight of this poetic delineation of truth, this unparalleled literary achievement. Stimulating influences were certainly not wanting. In the school of the Neoplatonists Augustine had learnt to flee the barren steppes of Aristotelian and Stoic psychology, and to fix his attention on mind and character, impulse and will. A great teacher—his own master, Ambrose of Milan—again, had introduced him to a new world of emotion and observation. But his 'Confessions' are none the less entirely his own. No forerunner threatens the claim of this undertaking to originality. It has, indeed, been observed that there is a morbid strain in the book, that he has made a stage-play of his bleeding heart, and it is true that in many places he seems to us over-strained, unhealthy, or even false ; but if we remember in what an age of depraved taste and lying rhetoric he wrote, we shall justly wonder that he has raised himself so high above the foibles of the time.

As the very conception of Augustine's book was new, so also was its execution and language. Not only is the force of his observation admirable, but equally so is the force of his diction. In the language of the 'Confessions' there meets us an inexhaustibly rich individuality, dowered at once with the irresistible impulse and faculty to express what it feels. Goethe makes his Tasso use the sad and proud saying :

> "Though other men are in their torments dumb,
> Me God permits to say how much I suffer."

This is true equally of Augustine. But not only of his sufferings was he able to speak. It was given to him to trace every motion of his heart in words, and above all, to lend speech to the pious mind and to intercourse with God. Of the power of sin and of the blessedness of the heart that hangs on God, he has been able so to speak that even to-day every tender conscience must understand his language. Before him, Paul and the Psalmists alone had thus spoken; to their school Augustine, the pupil of the rhetoricians, went to learn : and thus arose the language of the ' Confessions.' It is not difficult to dissect it into its component parts, to discriminate the Biblical element from the rhetorical, and to point out much that is far-fetched, and archaic —frigid conceits and artificial turns. But that which strikes us to-day as strange, or even occasionally as painful, is richly compensated by the highest merits. Admirable, above all, is the use of sayings and ideas from Holy Writ. Through the position which he gives them, he lends to the most insignificant words something striking or moving. In that great literary art, the art of giving to a well-known saying the most effective setting, he has surpassed all others.

Wonderful also is his power of summing up the phenomena of life and the riddles of the soul in short maxims and antitheses, or in pregnant sentences and new connotations. Much of the 'Confessions' has passed into the languages of the Western nations. We use much, or find much in our great writers like Lessing and Goethe, without thinking of its origin. 'The dumb chatterers,' 'victorious garrulity,' 'the biter bit,' 'the betrayed betrayers,' the 'hopeful young man,' the 'fetters of our mortality,' the 'rich poverty,' 'ignominious glory,' 'hateful gibberish,' 'life of my life,' and many similar images are either borrowed direct from Augustine, or can be traced back to him. But more important are his psychological descriptions and his maxims :—'That was my life—was it a life?'

' I became to myself a great problem,' ' Man is a deep abyss,' ' Peace of mind is the sign of our secret unity,' ' Every man has only his one Ego,' ' Every unordered spirit is its own punishment,' ' Every forbidden longing, by an unchangeable law, is followed by delusion,' ' You cannot do good without willing it, though what you do may in itself be good.'

These are a few isolated specimens ; it would be easy to go on for a long time with other examples. But he is much greater even than here in his connected descriptions. One example among hundreds must suffice. He pictures himself as wishing to rise to a vigorous Christian life, but held back by the lust of the world and by custom :

" Thus the burden of the world lay softly on me as on a dreamer, and the thoughts in which my senses turned towards Thee, my God, were like the efforts of those who would rouse themselves from sleep, but, overcome by the depth of slumber, ever sink back again. And when Thou calledst to me,

'Awake, thou that sleepest,' I would give thee no other answer than the words of delay and dream, 'Presently, but let me dream a little longer.' Yet the 'presently' had no end, and the 'yet a little longer' lengthened evermore."

Great as is his art, he never destroyed the uniformity of his style, which is from one fount, because dominated by a single rounded personality. It is a *person* that meets us in his language, and we feel that this person is everywhere richer than his expression. This is the key to the understanding of the enduring influence of Augustine. Life is kindled only upon life, one lover inflames the other: these are his own words, and we may apply them to himself. He was far greater than his writings, for he understood how by his writings to draw men into his life. And with all the tenderness of feeling, with all the constant melting into emotion and the lyricism of the style, there is yet a sublime repose throughout the work. The motto of the book—" Thou, Lord, hast made us after Thine own image, and our heart cannot be at rest till it finds rest in Thee "—is at the same time the seal of the book and the key-note of its language. No fear, no bitterness thenceforward troubles the reader; and that though the book is a sketch of the history of distress and inner trouble. " Fear is the evil thing," says Augustine in one place; but he talks with God fearlessly as with a friend. He has not ceased to see riddles everywhere— in the course of the world, in man, in himself; but the riddles have ceased to oppress him, for he trusts that God in His wisdom has ordered all things. Mists of sorrow and of tears still surround him, but at heart he is free. The impression, then, that the book leaves, may be compared with the impression we receive when, after a dark and rainy day, the sun at length gains the victory, and a mild ray lightens the refreshed land.

But the wonderful form and the magical language of the book are not, after all, its most important characteristics. It is the content, the story he tells, that gives it its real value. As a record of facts, the book is poor indeed. It paints the life of a scholar who grew up under conditions then normal, who had not to contend with adverse fortune or want, who absorbs the manifold wisdom of his time, and accepts a public office in order at last, with scepticism and dissatisfaction, to hand himself over to a holy life of resignation, to theological science, and to the firm-based authority of the Church. It was a course of development such as not a few of Augustine's contemporaries passed through. No other outlet, indeed, was then possible to piety and a serious scientific mind. If we conceive the story of Augustine from this point of view, we can get rid of a widespread prejudice, for the existence of which, it is true, he is himself to some degree responsible.

In wide circles the 'Confessions' are viewed as the portrait of a Prodigal Son, of a man who, after a wild and wasteful career, suddenly comes to himself and repents, or else as the picture of a heathen who, after a life of vice, is suddenly overcome by the truth of the Christian religion. No view can be more mistaken. Rather do the 'Confessions' portray a man brought up from youth by a faithful mother in the Christian, that is, in the Catholic, faith; who yet, at the same time, from his youth, by the influence of his father and of the mode of culture into which he was plunged, received an impulse towards the highest *secular* aims. They depict a man on whose mind from childhood the name of Christ has been ineffaceably imprinted, but who, as soon as he is roused to independent thought, is informed by the impulse to seek *truth*. In this effort, like us all, he is held down by ambition, worldliness, and sensuality; but he struggles unceasingly against them. He wins, at last, the victory over self, but in doing so he sacrifices his freedom of purpose to the authority of the Church, because in the message of this

Church he has experienced the power of breaking with the world and devoting himself to God.

In his external life this change presents itself as a breach with his past ; and it is in this view that he has himself depicted it. To him there is here nothing but a contrast between the past and the present. But in his inner life, in spite of his own representations, everything appears to us a quite intelligible development. It is true—and we understand the reason—that he was unable to judge himself in any other way. No one who has passed from inner unrest to peace, from slavery to the world to freedom in God and dominion over himself, can possibly, in surveying the path he trod in the past, call it the way of truth. But others, both contemporary and later, may judge differently ; and in this case such a judgment is made specially easy. For the man who here speaks to us is, against his will, compelled to give evidence that, even before his conversion, he strove unceasingly after truth and moral force ; and, on the other hand, the numerous writings he produced immediately after his ' break with the past,' prove that that break was by no means so complete as the ' Confessions '—written twelve years afterwards — would have us believe. Much of what only came to maturity in him during those twelve years, he has unconsciously transferred to the moment of conversion. At that time he was no ecclesiastical theologian. Spite of his resolve to submit himself to the Church, he was still living wholly in philosophical problems. The great break was limited entirely to worldly occupations and to his renunciation of the flesh ; the interests that had hitherto occupied his mind it did not affect. Thus it is not hard to refute Augustine out of Augustine, and to show that he has in his 'Confessions' antedated many a change of thought. Yet, at bottom, he was right. His life, essentially, had but two periods—one, that which he paints in the words, " In distraction I fell to pieces bit by bit, and lost myself in the Many "; the other, that in which he found in God the strength and unity of his being.

The former of these periods lies before us in his ' Confessions.' These have been repeatedly compared with those of Rousseau and Hamann, but really belong to a totally different class. In spite of the most deep-seated differences, I can compare Augustine's book with no other except Goethe's ' Faust.' In the ' Confessions ' we meet a living Faust, whose end is, of course, not that of the Faust of the poem. There is much affinity between the two, nevertheless. All those anguished revelations in the early scenes of ' Faust,' from the " Alas, I have explored Philosophy," to the resolve on suicide (" Say thy firm farewell to the sun") appear in the 'Confessions.' With heart-stirring emphasis Augustine cries again and again, " O truth, how the very marrow of my soul sighs after thee !" How often, like Faust, does he complain that the "hot struggle of eternal study" has left him no wiser than before. How often does he compassionate his pupils that he, a drunken teacher, has given them the wine of error. How painfully, too, falls from his lips the confession—" And now, to feel that nothing can be known, this is a thought that burns into my heart." " Could dog, were I a dog, so live?" says Faust; and Augustine, with the most savage envy, envies the ragged but cheerful beggar. He too, " to magic, with severe and patient toil, has now applied, despairing of all other guide, that from some spirit he may hear deep truths, to others unrevealed, and mysteries from mankind sealed"; and in his soul, too, there rises the enticing question, "whether Death, when it dissolves all feeling, dissolves and takes away all sorrows too."

Even the solution which Goethe gives to his poem, the way by which Faust attains release, is not quite without its parallel in Augustine. Faust, we read, is saved by heavenly love :

> " Upward rise to higher borders !
>   Ever grow, insensibly,
>   As, by pure eternal orders,
>   God's high presence strengthens ye :
>   Such the Spirit's sustentation,
>   With the freest ether blending ;
>   Love's eternal revelation
>   To Beatitude ascending."

And again :

> " As, up by self-impulsion driven,
>   The tree its weight suspends in air,
>   To love, almighty love, 'tis given
>   All things to form, and all to bear."

All this is precisely in the spirit of
Augustine ; and the idea of the wonderful
concluding scene of the second part of Faust
rests on one of his conceptions, little as Goethe
was conscious of the fact. It is unlikely that
Goethe had any direct acquaintance with
Augustine ; he probably knew him only at
secondhand. That in this world of illusion
and error, love, *divine* love, alone is strength
and truth ; that this love alone, in fettering,
frees and blesses—this is the fundamental
thought of the ' Confessions ' and of most of

Augustine's later works. The righteousness which avails with God is the love with which He fills us; and therefore the beginning of love, which is righteousness, is the beginning of blessedness, and perfected love is perfected blessedness. Such is the knowledge to which the struggling philosopher has attained, after seeking in vain elsewhere for rest and peace.

Nevertheless, there is a great gulf between the Faust of the poem and this Faust of reality. The former, in all his struggles, stands with a foot firmly planted on this earth. The God who has given him over for the time being to the devil, is not the good for the possession of which he strives; the inner battle with one's own weakness and sin is scarcely hinted at. To Augustine, on the contrary, the strife for truth is the strife for a supernatural good, for the holy and the high—in a word, for God. It is for this reason that the conclusion of Faust has about it an air of strangeness; we are in no degree prepared for this sudden turn. In Augustine the conclusion follows by an inner

K

necessity. His wanderings prove to be the very paths along which he has been led directly to this aim—blessedness through divine love.

Let us, in a few touches, draw a picture of these paths. Interesting in themselves, they are further interesting because they are typical of the time. Augustine entered into the closest sympathy with all the great spiritual forces of his age. His personality became actually enlarged till it embraced that of the whole existing world; and his individual advance therefore shows us how that world passed from heathenism and philosophy into Catholicism.

Born at Tagasta, a country town of Northern Africa, Augustine showed as a boy good but not brilliant capacity. After he had studied in the school of his native town and at Madaura, his father with some difficulty found the means to have him educated at Carthage. This father was in the ordinary way respectable, but weak in character, and in his private life not free from reproach. He had no higher

aim for his son than a career of worldly pros-
perity. He was himself a heathen; but his
wife was a Christian—a relation not uncommon
in the middle of the fourth century; it was
the women who spread Christianity in the
family. To his mother Augustine has raised
a noble monument, not only in his 'Confessions,' but elsewhere in his works. He
tells how she taught him to pray, and with
what passion he drank in her lessons: often, he
tells us, he fervently prayed to God that at
school he might escape the ferule. Later in
life he recalled how as a boy, in the delirium
of fever, he cried out furiously for baptism;
and, in all his wanderings, one relic of childhood remained with him never to be ex-
tinguished—reverence for Christ. Again and
again in his 'Confessions' he tells us that
all wisdom left him unsatisfied that was
not somehow connected with the name of
Christ. Thus the recollections of youth
became of the highest significance to the
man. Faust says :

> " O once, in boyhood's happy time, Heaven's love
> Showered down upon me, with mysterious kiss
> Hallowing the stillness of the Sabbath day !
> Yearnings for something that I knew not of,
> Deep meanings in the full tones of the bells."

How often, with wonderful variations, is this same thought heard resounding in the ' Confessions ' of Augustine !

Till the boy's seventeenth year imagination and youthful pleasure predominated in his mind. He had at first little taste for learning, although he mastered his lessons with ease. His only delight was to joke and play with his friends. To his mother's grief, also, he early fell into the sins of youth—sins which to his father and to society were no sins at all. At this time, in Carthage, one of Cicero's writings, the ' Hortensius,' came into his hands ; and it is from this moment that he reckons the beginning of a new and higher effort. The ' Hortensius ' no longer exists ; but we can clearly make out its spirit from the remaining works of the man : a high moral flight, a serious interest in the pursuit of truth, but on an uncertain foundation, stimulating rather than strengthening the principles; a book well adapted to wean a youthful mind from the wild life of a student to introspection and the study of the highest questions. And this it actually accomplished for Augustine; he severed himself henceforward from his boon companions, in order with absolute devotion to search for truth. But the book gave him no power over his sensual desires; and he soon found that he had outgrown a tuition which did not satisfy his understanding, left his religious feeling still hungry, and gave him no power of self-mastery. He had learned to know Cicero, the philosopher and moralist, and had become no better than before. But what Cicero did for him—leading him from an empty and trifling existence to serious self-examination and to the search for truth—moralists like Cicero did for the world of that time generally. Augustine remained, as the earliest books he wrote as a Catholic Christian prove, far more powerfully and permanently influenced than he is willing to allow. He now turned to Manichæism, a doctrine which then exercised a great attraction on the deeper spirits. Anyone who had gained some impressions from the contents of the Bible, but held the ecclesiastical interpretation of the Bible as a false one—especially if he could not surmount the stumbling-blocks of the Old Testament; anyone who was determined to cast aside leading-strings and examine things freely for himself; anyone who sought to know what inner principle holds the world together; anyone who strove from the physical to grasp the constitution of the spiritual world and the problem of evil—became in those days a Manichæan. Again, this sect, partly from necessity, partly by an inward impulse, surrounded itself like our freemasons with secrets, and formed at the same time a firm inner ring within the society of the age. Finally, its members exhibited a serious way of life; and the neophyte, in mounting step

by step to ever higher and narrower circles,
found himself at last in a company of saints
and redeemers. Into this society Augustine
entered, and to it he belonged for the nine
years preceding this twenty-eighth year of
his life. What attracted him to it was the
fact that it allowed Christ a high rank,
and yet assured to its disciples a reasonable
solution of the riddle of the world. Hungry as
he was, he flung himself greedily upon this spiritual nourishment. The doctrine that evil and
good are alike physical forces—that the struggle
in man's breast is only the continuation of
the great struggle in nature between light
and darkness, sun and cloud—struck him as
profound and satisfactory. In place of a
shallow ethic he found here a deep meta-
physic. Nevertheless, after but a few years
—he had meanwhile become a professor in
Carthage—he began to have his doubts. It
was the astrological knowledge, which he had
sought along with the metaphysical, that first
appeared to him as mere deception. Next,

a deeper study of Aristotle sobered his view of the Manichæan physics. His clear intelligence began to perceive that the whole Manichæan wisdom reposed on a physical mythology. The inborn turn of his mind towards the experimental and real gained the victory as soon as it was reinforced by the influence of Aristotle, the great logician and natural scientist of the ancient world. It was he that led back Augustine, like so many before and after, to a calm and sober thinking. Of all fables, the Manichæan now seemed to him the worst, because absolutely nothing in the world of the actual corresponds to them. But the actual was his aim ; and he made no secret of his rising doubts to his brethren in the society. At the time there was living in Rome a renowned Manichæan teacher, named Faustus. The friends who found themselves unable to solve the doubts of Augustine consoled him with the name of Faustus. "Faustus will make it all right," they said ; "Faustus will come and explain it all." Augustine allowed himself to be thus consoled for some time. At last, however, Faustus came in the flesh. The only section of the 'Confessions' over which lies a breath of humour, is that in which is painted the belauded Faustus, the perfect drawing-room professor, who yet was honest enough to confess, when Augustine alone was by, his own ignorance. Thenceforward, in his heart of hearts, Augustine was done with Manichæism.

But what next? Aristotle, it is true, had brought emancipation; but he was able to give no hint upon the questions to which Augustine sought an answer. It was here that Augustine began again to draw near the Church. But the Church forbade free inquiry; she maintained the fables of the Old Testament; she proclaimed, as Augustine thought, a God with eyes and ears, and made Him out to be the creator of evil. It was impossible that she should be the depositary of truth. Then, he decided, there can be no truth at all ; we must doubt everything. To this view he now resigned his soul, and fortified it by the reading of sceptical philosophers. He sought for a ready-made truth, and yet was unwilling to stifle his restless longing for it. No wonder that he fell into scepticism ; he felt himself, in his heart of hearts, poor and without a stay. Yet more, he had long laid upon himself the obligation to cast aside all immorality and obtain entire dominion over himself : an aim which, as he himself unwillingly confesses, he did in some regards attain. To the common frivolities and trivialities, to the theatres and plays, he had bidden farewell ; and he was conscientious in the discharge of his professorial duties. But the love of fame and of honour among men was a different matter ; and above all he was unable to free himself from a connection which he already regarded as immoral. Little as it contravened the social laws of the age, to him this relation caused a deep breach and cleavage in his personality. He saw himself severed from the good and holy, and from God ; in spite of all his good resolutions, he saw himself entangled with the world and with sensuality ; and, as he confesses later, he *would* not let himself be healed, because his sickness was dear to him. Yet, as in his serious contemporaries, pure moral feeling and artificiality even then were in him closely interwoven. A holy life appeared to him to be nothing but a life of most utter renunciation ; and to lead such a life he was still without the strength. In these perplexities, and in the mood of a sceptic, he left Carthage in order to work in Rome as a professor of rhetoric. The Carthaginian students with their loose manners had given him a distaste for his native Africa. But in Rome also he had some bad experiences with his pupils, and accordingly but a few months passed before he took a public professorship at Milan. The Manichæans, with whom he still maintained constant relations, since "nothing better had as yet appeared," had secured him this post by their recommendations to the influential Symmachus.

Here in Milan the transformation was at last completed, slowly it is true, but with extraordinary transparency and dramatic sequence. Augustine recognised with growing clearness that man can gain a solid hold in the highest questions only by serious unintermitting self-discipline; and he was now to prove that man gains moral force by freely giving himself up to a personality far surpassing his own. In Milan he met Bishop Ambrose. Hitherto he had fallen in with no Catholic Christian capable of impressing him. Such a one he was now to know. If at first it was perhaps the kindliness and extraordinary eloquence of Ambrose that captivated him, it was soon the matter of the Bishop's sermons that drew his attention. He himself tells us in the ' Confessions ' that the highest service Ambrose did him was to remove the stumbling-blocks of the Old Testament. Certainly the Greek method of interpretation, of which Ambrose was an exponent, exerted a strong influence on Augustine as on every cultivated mind of the age. But the really dominating force in Ambrose was the personality that lay behind his words. It was here that Augustine broke openly with Manichæism. If truth is to be found anywhere, it must be in the Church; to this acknowledgment he was brought by the influence of the great Bishop. The picture of Christ which his mother had been the first to show him, rose again before his soul, and he never afterwards lost it.

But Ambrose had no time to trouble himself about a man who, though he would willingly have believed, was nothing but a sceptic; and even yet there remained a fundamental stumbling-block to be removed. Augustine could not bring himself to believe that there can be an active spiritual being without material substance. The *spiritual* conception of God and the idealistic view of the world seemed to him unprovable, impossible. But while he thus struggled in vain for certainty, his despair at-finding himself still a slave to the world and sense, and unable to attain the mastery over himself, was much deeper than before. Fear of his Judge and fear of death lay like a dead-weight on his soul. He thirsted for *strength*; already he would have given all for this—honour, calling, nay even understanding itself. But like the sleeper that strives to rise, he sank back again and again. The most various plans fluttered before his mind : along with congenial friends and pupils, he hugged himself in the idea of withdrawing altogether from the world, and living, far from the madding crowd, a common life of personal training and of the search for truth. But the decision had as yet no force ; its execution was hindered by the calls of wife and business. What *essentially* he was already seeking in his theoretical and practical doubts was but one thing—intercourse with the living God, who frees us from sin. But God did not appear to him, and he did not find Him.

Help came to him from an unexpected quarter. He was reading some writings of the Neoplatonic school—a school in which Greek philosophy spoke its last word, and uttered its last testament. Like a dying man who only under compulsion, in the midst of his agonies, busies himself with the things of this world, Greek philosophy directed all her thoughts to the highest, to the holy, to God. Everything lofty and noble that she had gained in the course of a long toil, she compacted into a bold idealistic system, and a practical direction to the holy life. In Neoplatonism she taught that we must follow the authority of revelation, and that there is only *one* reality, God, and only *one* aim, to mount up to Him ; that evil is nothing but separation from God, and the world of sense only an unreal appearance ; that we can only attain to God by self-discipline and self-restraint, by contemplation ever rising from lower to higher spheres, and finally by an indescribable intoxication, an 'ecstasy,' in

which God Himself embraces the soul and
sends His light upon her :

> "All things transitory
> But as symbols are sent :
> Earth's insufficiency
> Here grows to event :
> The Indescribable,
> Here it is done."

These concluding words of 'Faust' are
Neoplatonism all over. The Neoplatonic
philosophy had more and more renounced the
'dry light' of science ; it had thrown itself
into the arms of revelation, in order to raise
men above themselves. This, the last product
of the proud Greek mind, did not disdain even
Christian writings in its desire to learn from
them. St John's Gospel was read and highly
valued in Neoplatonic circles. It was in this
philosophy that Augustine now steeped
himself ; it was this that solved for him his
theoretical riddles and doubts ; it was this
that drew him out of scepticism and sub-
jugated him for ever. The reality of spiritual
values, the spiritual conception of God, became

for him now a certainty. The keen criticism
which he formerly had applied to the theoretical groundwork of philosophical systems here
failed him. Scepticism had dulled his critical
faculty ; or rather—he sought above all for
guidance to the blessed life, and for an
authority which might guarantee to him the
living God. What he sought he transferred
to the new philosophy : for the holy being to
which he wished to give himself up, and whose
nearness he wished to feel, was not, as he
imagined it, given to him by Neoplatonism.
The true difference he did not fail to see ; but
in its deepest meaning he penetrated it neither
now nor later. That there existed a philosophy on to which he could fasten what his
soul longed for, was to him important before
all else. Neoplatonism became to him, as
to many before and after, a pathway to the
Church ; by its means he acquired confidence
in the fundamental ideas of the ecclesiastical
theology of the time. It is remarkable how
speedily, how imperceptibly he passed from

Neoplatonism to the recognition of the Bible
in its entirety and of the Catholic doctrine ;
or rather, how he came to see Neoplatonism
as true, but not as the whole truth. There
was wanting to it, above all, *one* item—the
recognition of redemption through the
incarnate God, and thereby the right way to
truth. These philosophers, said he, see the
Promised Land like Moses, but they know
not how to enter in and possess it. This he
fancied that he now knew : by the subjection
of the understanding to Christ. But Christ,
as he had learnt from Ambrose, is only where
the Church is. We must therefore *believe*,
and believe what the Church believes.
Augustine in his ' Confessions ' allows us no
doubt that the *decision* to submit ourselves
to authority is the condition of the attainment
of the truth. This decision he made, and
thus became a Catholic Christian. In this
inner transformation the causes are wonderfully
linked together—the Neoplatonic influence,
the enduring impression of the Person of

Christ, strengthened by the perusal of Paul's Epistles, and the grand authority of the Church.

He was now a Catholic Christian by conviction and will; but he himself describes his state of mind in the words: "Thus I had found the pearl of great price, but I still hesitated to sell all I had; I delighted in the law of God after the inward man, but I found another law in my members." No theory, no doctrine, could here avail him : only overpowering personal impressions could subject him or carry him away. And such impressions arrived. First, it was the news of a famous heathen orator in Rome, who had suddenly renounced a brilliant career and publicly professed himself a Catholic; a report that stirred him to his depths. Then, a few days later, a fellow-countryman, happening to visit him, told him an event that had recently taken place in Trèves. A few young imperial officials had gone a walk in the gardens on the city-walls, and

there fallen upon the hut of a hermit. In
the hut they found a book, the Life of St
Antony. One of them began to read it;
and the book exerted such a fascination upon
them that they forthwith resolved to leave
all and follow Antony. The narrator told
this story with flaming enthusiasm; he had
himself been present and a witness of the
sudden transformation. He did not see
what an impression his tale made on his
listener. A fearful struggle arose in
Augustine's mind: "Where do we allow
ourselves to drift? Why is this? The unlearned take the kingdom of heaven by force,
and we with our heartless learning still
wallow in flesh and blood!" In the conflict
of his feelings, no longer master of himself,
he flung into the garden. The thought of
that which he was to renounce struggled in
him with the might of a new life. He
fainted; and only awoke to consciousness
as he heard in a neighbouring house a child's
voice, probably in play, repeating again and

again the words, 'Take and read, take and read.' He hurried back to the house, and, remembering the story of St Antony, opened his Bible. His eye fell on the passage in Romans, "Not in rioting and drunkenness, not in chambering and wantonness, not in strife and envying ; but put ye on the Lord Jesus Chirst, and make not provision for the flesh, to fulfil the lusts thereof." "I would not read further, nor was there need ; for as I finished the passage there immediately streamed into my heart the light of peaceful certainty, and all the darkness of indecision vanished away." At this moment he broke with his past : he felt in himself the power to renounce the sinful habit, and to lead a new and holy life in union with his God. This he vowed to do, and kept his vow.

A proof that it was an *inner* transformation which he had undergone lies in the fact that while he thenceforward renounced his wife and his public occupation as an evil, he in no degree for the present gave up his studies or the circle of his interests. So far from it, that he removed with his friends and his mother to an estate near Milan, in order there to devote himself undisturbed to philosophy and to serious intercourse with his companions, and to pursue his philosophical speculations as he had pursued them hitherto. His ideal and that of his friends was not St Antony, but a society of wise men, as conceived by Cicero, Plotinus, and Porphyry. No obtrusive Church dogmas as yet disturbed the philosophical dialogues of the friends; but their minds were ruled by a sure belief in the living God; and in place of the old uncertainties about the starting-point and aim of all knowledge of truth, they now lived in the assurance given by the revelation of God in Christ and by the authority of the Church. The question whether happiness is secured by the search for truth or by the possession of truth, was mooted by Augustine in the circle of these friends, and decided in favour of the latter hypothesis. He resolved to pursue his unceasing investigations further; but the last and highest truth he *sought* no more, convinced that he had found it in subjection to the authority of God as proclaimed by the Church.

In this narrative I have attempted to follow the 'Confessions,' and only toward the end have I corrected their representations from those more trustworthy sources, the books written by Augustine immediately after his conversion. You will not have failed to feel the problem offered by this life. On the one side, a development from within outward by incessant toil, an ascent from a fettered and distracted existence to freedom and stability in God; on the other, the development into the belief laid down by authority, repose upon the Church, and the monkish conception of marriage and work. Even if we keep in mind the state of the times, how strange is it nevertheless that this rich and untiring spirit, striving after personal Christian piety, should only attain it by submitting to the authority of the Church !

These two things are henceforward inseparably interwoven in Augustine's life and thought. On the one side he speaks in a new fashion—but on the lines of the Church—of God and divine things. From the experience of his heart he witnesses of sin and guilt, repentance and faith, God's power and God's love. In place of a sterile morality he sets up a living piety, life in God through Christ. To this life he summons the *individual*; he shows him how poor and wretched he is, with all his knowledge and all his virtue, so long as he is not penetrated by the love of God. He shows him that the natural man is swayed by selfishness, that selfishness is slavery and guilt, and that every man is by nature a link in an infinite chain of sin. But he also teaches him that God is greater than our heart, that the love of God as revealed in Christ is stronger than our natural impulses, and that freedom is the blessed necessity of what is good. Wherever in the following millennium and later the struggle has arisen against a mechanical piety, self-righteousness, or jejune morality, there the spirit of Augustine has been at work. But, at the same time, no one before Augustine has, in so decided and open a fashion, established Christianity on the authority of the Church, or confused with the authority of institutions the *living* authority of saintly persons, who engender a life like their own.

The forces which were inseparably conjoined in his own experiences and life have continued to affect the Church through his influence ; his significance in the formation of Catholic ecclesiasticism and in the rule of the Church is no less than his *critical* significance, or than the power given him to arouse *individual* piety and *personal* Christianity.

The solution of this problem I shall not here attempt ; it must suffice to observe that fundamentally it is by no means astonishing. Religion and the faith dependent on authority,

M

different as they are, are severed by a narrow partition ; and, where faith is imagined as first of all a matter of knowledge, the partition vanishes entirely. At this point Luther stepped in and undertook to establish the Christian on a foundation from which he must view the authority of institutions, and monasticism, as a degenerate form of belief.

But every age has received from God its content, and every spirit its measure. Augustine's limits are at the same time his strength and the conditions of his activity. Within his limitations, in the forty-three years of his Catholic life, he raised himself to a personality whose sublimity and humility are amazing to us. A stream of truthfulness, kindness, and benevolence, and on the other hand of living ideas and deep conceptions, runs through his writings, by means of which he became the great teacher of the West. True, he was left behind at the Reformation, though that very Reformation he helped to call into existence ; and his religious view of the world failed to hold its ground against the scientific knowledge to which we have since Leibnitz attained. True, Catholicism strove to stifle his still surviving influence at the Council of Trent, in the contest with Jansenism, and by the Vatican Decrees. But he is, in spite of all, no dead force ; what he has been to the Church of Christ will not vanish, and even to the Romish Church he will leave no rest.

From Easter 387 to Easter 1887 fifteen hundred years have passed since Augustine was baptised and started on the service of the Church. No one has celebrated the day ; no monument has been set up to the teacher of the Church. But he has the noblest of all memorials : his name stands written in imperishable characters on the leaves of Western history from the days of the great migrations to our own.

3 4711 00208 3774

LaVergne, TN USA
30 March 2011
222224LV00001B/60/P